THE GOOD EARTH OF AMERICA

The American Assembly, *Columbia University*

THE GOOD EARTH
OF AMERICA
PLANNING OUR LAND USE

Prentice-Hall, Inc., *Englewood Cliffs, New Jersey*

A SPECTRUM BOOK

Library of Congress Cataloging in Publication Data
MAIN ENTRY UNDER TITLE:

The Good earth of America.

(A Spectrum Book)
At head of title: The American Assembly, Columbia University.
Papers, prepared as background material for the Arden House Assembly on Land Use.
Includes bibliographical references.
1. Land—United States—Addresses, essays, lectures.
I. Harriss, Clement Lowell, ed. II. American Assembly.
HD205 1974.G65   333.7′0973   74–12007
ISBN 0–13–360347–4
ISBN 0–13–360339–3(pbk.)

10 9 8 7 6 5 4 3 2 1

PRENTICE-HALL INTERNATIONAL, INC. (*London*)
PRENTICE-HALL OF AUSTRALIA PTY., LTD. (*Sydney*)
PRENTICE-HALL OF CANADA, LTD. (*Toronto*)
PRENTICE-HALL OF INDIA PRIVATE LIMITED (*New Delhi*)
PRENTICE-HALL OF JAPAN, INC. (*Tokyo*)

Table of Contents

Preface

Since the day when, according to *Genesis*, "the Lord God took man and put him in the garden of Eden to dress it and keep it," people have responded in the course of everyday living as much to their physical surroundings as to the social, as much to land and the things on it as to other people. If it is true by another view that life began with water, it nonetheless rests on land, and the places where we live and work and play are central to our values.

Those of us who helped to plan this volume shared the editor's belief that many decisions about land use have greater long-range and longer lasting effects than most other private and governmental choices. And although it may very well be that what we are able to do with land depends in considerable measure on the decisions of the past, the choices we have yet to make will influence the way of life of our children. As the participants in the Arden House Assembly on Land Use said in April, 1974, "The decision-making process in American land use that has served the past will not serve the present and future. As we face new problems, we must think and act anew." We are learning the need to treat all land with more respect. Greater demands are now made on it by a growing and rapidly urbanizing population. And now we know that some of the most ecologically vulnerable and some of the most valuable, renewable resource lands have not been adequately protected.

The American Assembly believes that improvements in land use large enough to make a significant contribution to a better life can be achieved. Wherefore this book. Originally designed as background for the Arden House meeting (the report of which may be had from The American Assembly) the volume is also meant for the general reader, who, we are confident, will find in it facts and ideas, whether new or old, in new combination to enable him to take a fresh look at the good earth of America, the better to dress it, keep it, and rest upon it.

As a nonpartisan educational forum in current affairs, The American Assembly takes no official stand on the material it presents for public discussion. The ideas herein are those of the writers themselves and do not represent our position. Officially we have none. The Lincoln Foundation, which supported this national program in generous measure, should also be dissociated in the reader's mind from the views on these pages.

Clifford C. Nelson
President
The American Assembly

C. Lowell Harriss

Introduction

Everyone "uses" many parcels of land. Could anyone possibly envision the thousands of pieces of land which are involved in making available the goods and services we consume? Even the separate plots we touch in a day's living, including streets and other property owned by government, will add up to hundreds or thousands. Ownership differs. And so do other aspects—size, location, worth, topography, development, zoning, fertility, and so on.

By reasonable standards of expectation much of the location process has been done well. Private ownership and the many forces of the marketplace, competition and the lack thereof, along with processes of governmental regulation and ownership, have combined to produce results which are impressive, favorably so. The accomplishments of organization represent achievements of a high order.

Today, however, criticisms are frequent; and expressions of concern about land use are in the news. The thrust of apparent interest directs attention to what is not good—in actual conditions and even more so as indicated for the future. Things could be better now. And observed or feared trends give rise to apprehension. The future we are making for our later years, and for our children, will depend significantly upon land-use practices. The communities in which we live and work, and the areas for recreation, will be more or less satisfactory depending upon decisions yet to be made—and over which men and women today have control.

In ways that are important economically—and therefore humanely—land differs from other things we use for production or in consumption, from machinery for production to durable goods for consumption. The

Author of many books and articles on economics, C. LOWELL HARRISS *is Professor of Economics at Columbia University and economic consultant, Tax Foundation, Inc. In 1972–73 he was president of the National Tax Association-Tax Institute of America, and since 1972 he has been vice president of the International Institute of Public Finance. He has been a consultant to government and member of many public and private economic associations.*

aspects that make land different give rise to the need for special attention such as in this volume.

Land is fixed in quantity, not completely so but enough to make this a feature of importance in policies about how land is to be used. As population grows, in some particular locality or over the country as a whole, people must do something to adjust to the declining amount of land per capita. Paying more for land does not call more of it into existence.

To a large extent the physical characteristics of land result from what nature has done. In some contrast, what people will pay to use a piece of land, its price, depends upon conditions of the community and governmental investment. What will determine how much the owner can charge for use of a good location or for a plot of land which is attractive for one or more of several reasons? Whether he gets a lot or only a little will usually depend to a considerable extent on what others have done rather than on the inputs of labor and man-made capital put into making his parcel more attractive than when nature finished its work.

Rising incomes, population increase, and expectations of inflation have raised prices of much land rather strikingly. These higher prices can serve the valuable function of allocating limited areas for more, as against less, effective uses. Traditional forces of private ownership bring about this result. But objections to paying the high "toll" which market forces induce will contribute to arguments for changing land-use policies. We can expect pressures to substitute political (governmental) for market determination.

Today's explicit interest in land use reflects additional considerations. Two that are both weighty and complex grow out of uniqueness of land.

First: Some changes in land use are irreversible. To all intents and purposes, some drainage or inundation, some subdivision or consolidation, some shift from farm use to residential or factory-commercial use, will so commit the land, and the environment (broadly conceived), that much of what existed before will be gone beyond practical recall. The loss may sometimes be of irreplaceable and even unique elements. What must be given up will have great attractions to some people even though, obviously, the parties deciding on the change will have been willing to sacrifice what was lost for whatever they expect to obtain.

In other cases, probably the majority, irreversibility from change in use is not absolute. Earlier conditions can be restored. With investment of funds and resources—with determination, aesthetic and engineering talent, legal authority, and so on—what was desirable about some earlier aspects can be reproduced rather closely. But the costs will be very high. There may be alternatives, especially if the element of location is not of central importance for the "restoration"; the essence of the desired use may be realizable elsewhere. But the cost can in fact prevent achieving this result. Structures have lives of decades. Typically, the capital that goes on to land has such a long life that a new use is a commitment for one third or half of a century.

Some of the present, and properly increasing, desire for reconsideration of land-use policies grows out of the economic, political, ecological, engineering, and other realities that make many changes in the use of parcels of land so binding as to preclude practical reconsideration for a long time. A related aspect: the cost of doing something desirable in the future will be greater, perhaps very much so, because of lack of foresight now. Having many examples from the past of planning (or lack of real planning) which proved very poor indeed, should we not exert ourselves to meet the challenges?

Second: The belief that better policies can and should be devised reflects awareness of what economists call "externalities." The responsible concerns about land use grow in part out of the fact that what happens on one plot of land affects persons beyond those who make the decisions and bear the costs or share in the rewards. The addition of a beautiful new building, the failure to replace an eyesore, new highways or industrial plants, will affect those around.

If I keep a plot of urban or urban-fringe land in low-density use when others would pay "reasonably" to use it more fully, then they may have to settle farther out; day after day they will have to incur greater costs of time and resources in travel. The ability to put one plot to better use often requires assembly into a total of several parcels. No plot of land can be "an island unto itself." Relations among parcels of ground, each fixed in its place, are different from the relations among other types of property. The incentives of private property cannot serve all of the interests affected by decisions.

Recent discussions of ecology and problems of the environment have yielded many examples of effects which are external to (outside or beyond) particular parcels of property where a condition originates. Air and water pollution illustrate. The discharges from one place affect the desirability of properties downwind or downstream. An improvement in shopping or recreation or transportation facilities will add to the worth of properties around. Such effects are external to the decisions and to the transactions involving actual land uses and are termed "externalities."

Some of these external effects are desirable. Some are unwelcome. They do not get into the calculations on which decisions are made.

Private and governmental actions involving land use rest on considerations which do not include all of the results. Many externalities—"third party effects," "spillovers," "neighborhood results"—are by any reasonable standards too small to warrant concern in a world of human beings. Sometimes, too, both "goods" and "bads" will grow out of the same decisions so that a proper balance of the "outside-the-market" results would be difficult to assess. Economists writing about interdependent relations, and the bearings of one use of land on the neighboring parcels, may have given misleading impressions which confuse frequency with size.

Unquestionably, however, decisions to use land in one way or another can be of significance for private property owners operating under present rules. Can "we" do appreciably better than with existing procedures to take account of more of the total effects, i.e., of more of the realities than now enter into the calculations of those in the market?

One approach would attempt to induce or compel the parties to a transaction to bring the broader range of results into private decisions. This process is termed "internalizing" the "externalities." Buyers and sellers, users, and to some extent governments as tax collectors, would share more fully in the *total* of effects, good and bad, of choices about the use of land. The chapters in this volume touch on the issues at various points.

Proposals for improving land use frequently involve different, usually expanded, roles for government. The considerations which have influenced land use have always had some governmental element, not the least being taxes. Such has been true even where more specifically economic (market) forces have been dominant. Trying to judge the relative weight of political and economic elements which led to the land-use decisions made in settling this country, and in building its towns and cities, would not be useful here.

More to the point today will be the effort to learn how both sets of forces can be used to best advantage. Some of the more articulate exponents of reexamining—and recasting—land-use practices focus on changing the scope of political activity. Often they propose to enlarge it. Yet one set of criticisms of current realities grows out of dislike of the ways some groups of voters use political power. Zoning, for example, can be used to exclude certain land uses which others would prefer. Can we, as a practical reality, expect better results if local influences were subject to more state or federal direction?

A goal of expanded governmental influence would involve the attempt to recognize externalities more fully. In principle, governmental institutions can hope to take account of aspects of land use which even the best of private markets cannot be expected to deal with adequately. Can we not recognize the interrelations among plots of land? How many areas are doing as well as reasonably possible to prepare for the future?

Many states have established substantial programs to guide land use. Some local governments on their own, as well as under pressure from states, have acted. Numerous federal programs have direct and indirect effects on land. Through a land-use bill, described later in this volume, Congress would create inducements of considerable attraction for states to develop planning.

Early in the planning of this American Assembly it became clear that coverage would have to be limited. Space and time would not permit discussion of some highly important topics, to say nothing of many which though in a sense subsidiary can be of great significance. The selection does range broadly while dealing more completely with subjects which are clearly of prime importance—for untold millions as they will live their lives through decades to come.

Carl H. Madden

1

Land as a National Resource

How will we use our land in the future? One thing is clear. We can no longer live with the land-use policies of the past. The predominant policy has been one of unfettered economic growth—the development philosophy. At one time this philosophy served a useful purpose. It enabled almost everyone to live better.

But the development philosophy was flawed in two ways. Most advocates treated land as if it were indestructible. Secondly, they treated land merely as a commodity, ignoring its biological role as a crucial link in the web of life on earth.

More than a century ago, de Tocqueville saw our "boundless continent" as the basic source of strength for the new republic. Since then, the U. S. people have generally treated land as a commodity of limitless supply for private exploitation. Land could be divided and subdivided. Parcels could be owned by individuals who could use the land they owned in whatever ways they saw fit or sell it in the marketplace. Economic science explained this behavior with its theories of exchange, capital, and distribution.

But land is not indestructible. Treating land as merely a commodity rather than also as a natural and a community resource often led to its despoliation. Of course, the despoliation of the land and deterioration of the quality of life in the cities did not go unnoticed. Juxtaposed against the development thrust was the late 19th and early 20th century conservation movement, begun about when the frontier ended. And the conservation movement has been gaining strength as the development thrust has

CARL H. MADDEN, *chief economist for the U. S. Chamber of Commerce, has been economist for the Senate Banking and Currency Committee and consultant to the Treasury Department. In 1963 he was Dean of the College of Business Administration, Lehigh University. Dr. Madden has written several textbooks in economics and many economic studies.*

subsided. Added to the conservation movement in recent years is the new science of ecology, whose vantage point shows "the connectedness of things" in nature to be subtle, complex, and often not obvious to intuition.

We are forced by the widening of human perception through the power of new knowledge to rethink how we will use our land in the future. We can no longer rely solely on economic science for guidance since rigid adherence to the cause-effect, single-variable principles of the firm has burdened us with our present circumstances. How did that happen and where do we go from here?

America's Land and Its Uses

First, a word about the land itself. In 1970 the average person in the U. S. had the products and use of about eleven acres of land—some in western desert, some in Arctic tundra or barren mountaintops, but some in fertile cropland, magnificent forest, or the valuable land of our towns and cities. Land remains a great resource. Our total land surface per person is almost exactly the world average, but our land is vastly more productive than that of the world as a whole.

The "big three" of land use, in terms of acres, are grazing, forestry, and cropland, with 34, 32, and 23 percent respectively of the total area of the 48 contiguous states. Two other important uses of land—urban and recreation use—together account for 4 percent of the total area, but these uses directly affect far more people than the others. The five uses together comprise 93 percent of the total land area; the other 7 percent is used for water management and storage, transportation, mining, defense, or is idle land.

Land use will be affected in the future, as it has been in the past, by demographic, economic, and technical trends. From 205 million people in 1970, the U. S. may grow by an estimated 60 million to somewhat fewer than 300 million people by 2000, the exact size depending on whether the birth rate remains low. Land area remains about constant while population grows, since the fertility rate would have to stay at the zero population growth level of 2.1 children per family for 75 years before population growth would stop. By 1970, 73 percent of the U. S. population was urban, living on about 2 percent of the land area. The value as a whole of this 2 percent was approximately 50 percent greater than the value of all the other 98 percent.

In recent decades, the U. S. population has become more urbanized, more suburbanized, more metropolitanized, and more coastalized. That is, people are moving to towns and cities from rural areas. Within urbanized areas, people have been moving to suburbs. Thus, metropolitan populations grow faster than central city totals, and some very large cities have gotten smaller while their metropolitan area population has grown.

Finally, people have been moving out of the Midwest and rural areas to locations near the coasts. By 1970, half the population lived no more than 50 miles from a coast, including the Great Lakes coasts.

Economic and technical trends have both "shrunk" and "expanded" the size of the country. As man has developed a highly productive economy, communications and transportation have markedly shrunk the effective space of the U. S., in terms of allowing travel and freight shipments over long distances, and expanded it in the sense of opening up new areas for use of people living in various places. Moreover while the fraction of the total population living in metropolitan areas has grown very rapidly—and in this sense people are "crowded together in urban regions"—still, the average amount of land per person in urban regions has grown throughout the twentieth century.

The economic and social size of the nation, measured by the time distance across it, has shrunk. To illustrate, the shrinkage is as much as from a map the size of a moderately large dining room table (pre-railroad), to a map the width of four quarter coins (rail distance, 1912), to a map the width of one quarter (air distance, 1931), to a map half the width of a dime (piston air distance, 1950), and finally to a map the width of a kitchen match head (jet air distance today).

The highly productive economy, the urbanization of the population, and the shrinking of social and economic space have all led to growing concern over the quality of our environment. By and large, little attention has been given to the impact of the production process on the natural environment. But with the advent of nuclear power, the prospect of nuclear fusion, the increasing scale of many types of technology, the rapid growth in energy use and the use of chemical fertilizer, our past concentration on production for the consumer seems to more and more people to be misguided and incomplete. Of course, the matter of the environment goes far beyond land use. And it is far from clear that people are willing to pay for environmental costs. Still, it is becoming evident that past land-use policies will change.

Most of our land is, and will remain, privately owned. About one-third of our total land area, however, is publicly owned, largely by the federal government. Since Jefferson bought Louisiana from France for $15 million in 1803, the U. S. has expanded its territory immensely. We bought Florida from Spain in 1819; we annexed the independent Republic of Texas (after its war with Mexico) in 1845. We settled with Great Britain the boundary dispute over the Pacific Northwest in 1846. Then, after our own war with Mexico in 1848, we annexed the Pacific Southwest, including California, and later bought (in the Gadsden Purchase) from Mexico a large piece of southern Arizona. We bought Alaska in 1867 from Russia and annexed Hawaii in 1898.

Most of this land became the property of the U. S. government. For

100 years after the U. S. gained its independence, the dominant political philosophy was to dispose of the land to settlers. The Homestead Act of 1862 gave a settler (excluding blacks) up to 160 acres of land in turn for his residing on it for five years, making some improvements, and the payment of very modest fees. Other acts of Congress were equally or more generous. Sizable land areas were granted to states for public purposes such as to set up schools, to construct railroads, and to build canals and highways. The process of land disposal meant opportunity for Americans and dominated early American history. Heedless and headlong, it was a major social and political force throughout the nineteenth century, and it moved two-thirds of the land in the 48 coterminous states out of the public domain, mostly into private ownership. Land was the capital given to ordinary people by government.

Although most land will remain privately owned, government now has extensive powers over the use of private land. One is the power of eminent domain, to take private land needed for public purposes. Another is taxation (one of the largest costs of land ownership). A third is the police power (to impose zoning ordinances, to protect owners against nuisances, to set up subdivision rules). And, finally, there is the power of the public purse: to subsidize the building of highways and airports, power plants and power lines (especially in rural areas); or to help finance forest fire control, soil conservation, reduction of crop acreage, or other programs through payments to farmers.

Origins of the Commodity Concept of Land

In the process of rethinking land-use policy, it is important to look back at the origins of the concept of land ownership. A thousand years of Anglo-American history record the gradual accumulation of individual rights in land, encompassed in what is called "fee simple." Centuries of political struggle were required to get to the point where a holder in fee simple could theoretically do anything whatever with his possession.

The Anglo-American title system is descended from William the Conqueror who introduced continental feudalism to Saxon England in 1066. In concept, all land belonged to the sovereign; and he was in no way beholden to anyone else for his rights. He enfeoffed large tracts to major barons in return for promises of military service. The great barons, known as tenants-in-chief, sub-enfeoffed land to lesser barons and so on down the feudal chain to the knight's fee which was in theory enough land to support the knight and his horse. The practice never quite coincided with the concept.

Over many centuries, the whole system disintegrated as the individual rights of individual holders progressively encroached on the rights of the crown and of the great barons. Magna Carta was a step along the way.

Eventually, most of the land in Britain and virtually all of it in the United States was converted to "fee simple" title or some variant of it. Fee simple is often described as a "bundle of rights." As time went on the bundle got bigger until about the end of the nineteenth century when it crested.

But the issues in the struggle were political and economic. Until well into the nineteenth century, the word *scientist* did not exist; what we call scientists were known as "natural philosophers," and they comprised a small group, mostly amateurs and a few professors. Only around the turn of this century, with the rise of conservationists, were scientific arguments of biology and chemistry brought to bear on land-use policy. To the extent that earlier, the Crown embodied the concept of the general welfare in the feudal structure, modern society by paying note to natural and social science is marching back toward where it was once before. But to the extent that the general welfare is a concept never identified with the actual person of a monarch, the new direction can be a giant step forward.

Should land be property? In the seventeenth century, John Locke argued that it should:

> The great and chief end, therefore, of Men's uniting into Commonwealths, and putting themselves under government, is the Preservation of their Property. As much land as a man tills, plants, improves, cultivates, and can use the product of, so much is his property. He by his labour does, as it were, enclose it from the Common.

God commanded man to labor the earth and so entitled him to appropriate whatever land he mixed with his labor, and "there was still enough and as good [land] left, for others."

In parts of the world where land was already parceled out, Locke justified unlimited ownership of land on esoteric grounds as well as because it "quickened" and increased trade. Fundamentally, he argued that man had a natural right to own property. Indeed, "life, liberty, and property" almost got into the Declaration of Independence in 1776; Jefferson substituted "pursuit of happiness" only, as it were, at the last moment.

Whatever the arguments, the fact was that in the western world of the seventeenth century, individuals called land their own. It was a commodity to be exchanged in the marketplace. But what was its value? And how much of the national income should accrue to the landlord class? These questions preoccupied western economists of the eighteenth and nineteenth centuries.

LAND IN CLASSICAL ECONOMICS

One aspect of their concept of land is directly pertinent to the problem we face here today. Both the Physiocratic philosophers and the economists who developed classical economics saw land as a source of surplus value

over and above costs of production. All the emphasis was on the extent
and the bounty of the land. No thought was given to the possibility of
depletion or destruction of its value. No thought was given to the role of
land in the life cycle because nothing was known of the later scientific dis-
covery of the interrelatedness of all life in its terrestrial environment.

From the development of better plows in the Middle Ages, allowing
farmers to plow up extensive grass lands, farming technology improved.
Man saw himself for the first time as the master of nature. The theme
emerged that man could shape nature to his own ends through science.
But nature was viewed as a machine in the mechanistic view of scientists
and mathematicians such as Descartes, Galileo, and Newton. In the eighteenth century, the Physiocrat Robert Turgot said, ". . . It is the earth
which is always the first and only source of all wealth; it is that which as
the result of cultivation produces all the revenue." All surplus value came
from the land.

In Chapter II of his *Principles,* David Ricardo referred four times in
the first two pages to the "original and indestructible" powers of the soil
and once to the "inexhaustible" quantities of air and water. Thomas
Malthus too referred to rent as a surplus that we owed to "the bounty of
nature." And Alfred Marshall said,

> We may call to mind that the land has an inherent income of heat and light
> and air and rain, which man cannot greatly affect and advantages of situation,
> many of which are wholly beyond his control. . . . These are the chief of its
> properties, the supply of which is not dependent on human effort.

Clearly, the possibility of massive air and water contamination or in-
terruption of nature's life cycle was the furthest thing from their minds.
Quite the opposite—Marshall went on to argue that the properties of the
soil can be greatly improved by man's effort. All the emphasis was on
land's bounty and accretion to its value. Classical economics was thoroughly imbued with the mechanistic view of the mathematicians and
physicists of the eighteenth century. Indeed, up to today, economic theory
remains largely mechanistic. It pays little attention to the depletion of
resources or to the uses the consumer actually makes of the products and
services produced. Everything that reaches the consumer shows up again
in some form as a residual and eventuates in waste. However, economic
theory is able to deal with the problem of waste only episodically; the
problem is not integrated into economic theory as a major consideration.

The English economists' view of land's valuation and the distribution
of its product was useful for their time. Marshall argued that the theoretical division between rent and the tenant's share made capital funds available and spurred development. But we must keep in mind that all their
concern was focused on rural lands and land's agricultural possibilities.

In Marshall's time, the notion of land as a source of surplus value was abandoned in economic thought and land came to be viewed as simply another factor of production used in a complementary fashion with labor and capital to produce goods of value to consumers. Land took on a real, market value because of its combination with the other factors of production, and the focus shifted to its marginal productivity in combination with other factors. This marginal productivity gave it a capital value and clarified the intellectual perception of any given piece of land as real, private property. A German economist and landowner, J. H. V. von Thunen, began to develop the latter view of the valuation of a piece of real property as early as 1830. Others, working independently, later added to the theory of land valuation in neoclassical economics.

Not only was it necessary to relate the value of land to the product derived from it as the neoclassical economists did; it was also necessary to recognize that the product of land was a flow of goods and services and to factor that into the value equation. The result was the modern basis for many of the ideas in business finance.

For this dimension we may thank Messrs. Eugene von Bohm Bawerk and the American economist Irving Fisher, who first developed the theory of interest—although they did not fully agree upon why interest arose as a return to capital. On one thing they did agree: present goods are valued more highly than future goods, and the rate at which the value of future goods is discounted to transform it into present value is the rate of interest. The greater the rate of interest the lower the present value of the future amount at any given point in time. For example, at an interest rate of 10 percent, $10,000 payable thirty years from today is worth only $570 today while at a 5 percent rate of interest it is worth $2,310.

This view also implies a time horizon beyond which the present value of a future amount is negligible. For example, at a 10 percent rate of interest $10,000 payable five years from today is worth $6,210 today; $10,000 payable fifty years from today is worth only $850 today; and $10,000 payable 100 years from today is worth practically nothing. That means there is a finite time horizon on investment under the commodity concept of land.

The location of this time horizon is not a happenstance. It could be drawn closer by raising the interest rate. It goes to the heart of the valuation of capital, including land, and is determined by the conditions of supply and demand. On the supply side there is the time preference of savers who are the source of investment funds. On the demand side is the productivity of land and capital. The time preference of savers for present over future consumption has to be overcome by the interest rate that investors are prepared to offer them.

These ideas are the roots of contemporary business finance theory. This view is the basis upon which investments are made today. There is no meaningful distinction here between capital and land. Although this conclusion has been the source of great controversy even before the time of Alfred Marshall, land is seen as different from capital only in that it is a "free gift of nature" whereas capital is the result of man's efforts to produce. Yet land is allocated—its use is determined—by this microeconomic theory of investment. Many conservation investments would not begin to pay off in economic benefits for decades. Under the commodity concept of land, when such conservation investments would have to compete with other investment opportunities that would pay off sooner, they simply would not be undertaken. One has to go outside the economic paradigm to make certain conservation investments. One has to view land as a resource instead of as a commodity.

LAND AS CAPITAL IN THE UNITED STATES

The commodity view of land was an engine of economic growth, and growth has served us well. However, it has not been an unmixed blessing. When America was first colonized in the early seventeenth century land was abundant. Economic and social pressures emanating from the abundance of land in the New World quickened colonization and dictated land-use policies for two or more centuries.

For example, large areas of land were originally granted to aristocratic European families in Maryland, Pennsylvania, the Carolinas, New Jersey, Maine, and New Hampshire. William Penn held 47 million acres. Some of these families (not Penn) attempted to re-establish feudalism on their landed estates; but it did not work, because of the very abundance of land which made the effort possible in the first place. Immigrants would not work for a big landlord when they could easily acquire cheap and fertile land of their own.

And immigrants, too, were abundant. They were attracted by the prospect of available land. Land had a special status-giving characteristic for Europeans of those times, because it was the major form of wealth and independence. And the growing scarcity of land in England generated a flow of land-hungry peasants who had recently been displaced from their own lands by the enclosure movement. The enclosure movement itself probably resulted in great part because of the growing market economy and the effect of new markets for the produce of the land on the value of the land.

The British scholar C. K. Meek has told us how in "primitive" parts of Africa, land originally had no value or a vaguely conceived communal value. The land took on some characteristics of property when an individual cultivated a piece of it and it became "his" land in the eyes of his neighbors. At least it was his land for the time that he kept it tilled and cleared, after which—in an early escheat policy—it reverted to tribal ownership or simply lay fallow awaiting the next proprietor. But, as markets for the produce developed in Africa, cleared plots took on a greater economic worth. Boundaries became more important and better defined.

Is it not likely that ever since the origins of history this pattern of events has created the institution of landed property in most western societies? It is reasonable to think so. In this regard individualistic microeconomics serves us well in interpreting the institutions of the past. Private property takes on scarcity value like anything else: the greater the value, the better the boundaries must be defined.

The abundance of American land in the era of colonization determined the uses of land. Fertile land seemed unlimited in supply. The entirety of the continent east of the Mississippi was forested. Elementary economic production theory dictates that in an economically efficient production process the relatively abundant land should be used extensively—and it was used extensively (albeit without benefit of Marshallian production theory which was fully developed years afterward). Cotton and tobacco exhausted the lands of the South, but there was always the prospect of more land further west. Exploiting the soil was common and under the circumstances, good economics for the landowner. When erosion and exhaustion of nutrients despoiled the land, there was no attempt to restore fertility. It was cheaper to clear a new and more fertile area.

The view that land was like any other form of private capital shaped most land-use policy in the United States up through the middle of the twentieth century. Homesteading has been one of our most durable land-use policies. Much of the original colonial lands were distributed to ordinary people. In 1664 New Jersey began giving 150 acres of land to each freeman who could find transportation to the colony. The Dutch West India Company followed the same practice in New York. Similarly, the Virginia Company distributed its Middle Atlantic lands by headrights for each member of an immigrant's family. In many of the colonies the land was sold off in small holdings by the original companies. But the effect on land tenure was the same, and the pattern was set. Individual ownership and use of land was the rule. And exploitation of the land was the rule as well since land was so abundant in those times.

The perception of rural land as a nearly free good in comparison with the value of other factors of production persisted into the nineteenth century. Under the authority of the 1862 Homestead Act, the 160 acres of western land given to many bona fide settlers was seen as assuring opportunity in an almost empty subcontinent. Under the terms of the Timber Culture Act, 160 acres were given to anyone promising to plant 10 acres in timber. Western grazing lands were sold off at 25 cents per acre under the 1877 Desert Land Act. Under the 1878 Timber and Stone Act, lands valuable only for timber and stone were sold in units of up to 160 acres for $2.50 per acre.

Then there was mining. Under the Mining Act of 1872 any individual could stake a claim on federal lands which he could then use or sell as he chose. In *The Quiet Crisis,* Stewart Udall tells us of the effect of mining on the value of land. In 1852, Anthony Chabot, a California goldminer, devised a canvas hose and nozzle that would wash banks of gold-bearing gravel into placer pits for processing. The end result was massive movement of soil into the rivers draining the Sierra Nevada. Communities were inundated with muck; valley farms were covered with gravel. Strip mining too was carried forward under the presumption that land was abundant and therefore cheap. But as we know now—land is not indestructible, and it is scarce and valuable.

THE INDIAN CONCEPT OF LAND

The early American view of land use was in direct opposition to the American Indians' concept of land and how it should be treated. The Indian was close to the land but not in the sense that one is tied by property rights. The Indian's attachment was a deep, emotional tie. He intuitively saw himself and the land as integral parts of a larger whole. Contrary to the large scale raising of cash crops by itinerant farmers who moved from farm to farm seeking more fertile soil, the Indians were often rooted to their land and had an early appreciation for the sources of plant nutrients to restore the productive powers of the soil.

When approached to negotiate for the transfer of their lands to the state, the Indians were dumbfounded. In the words of Chief Sealth of the Duwamish Tribe in the state of Washington, as he wrote to President Pierce in 1855:

> How can you buy or sell the sky—the warmth of the land? The idea is strange to us. Yet we do not own the freshness of the air or the sparkle of the water. How can you buy them from us? We will decide in our time. Every part of this earth is sacred to my people. Every shining pine needle, every sandy shore, every mist in the dark woods, every clearing and humming insect is holy in the memory and experience of my people. . . . The air is precious to the redman. For all things share the same breath—the beasts, the trees, the man. . . .

Yet the Indians were forced to negotiate and accept the Anglo-American concept of land use. For example, the Cherokee Nation once spanned areas of North and South Carolina, Georgia, Alabama, and Tennessee. As settlers moved in, some Cherokees moved on to Arkansas to find escape. But most did not move. The Eastern Cherokees agreed to cede their lands to the United States and emigrate to an Oklahoma reservation in return for $5 million. Some were hesitant. In the euphemistic words of a 1924 law treatise, "The Western Cherokee manifested great reluctance to emigrate and it became necessary to send troops into their country to secure their removal."

In 1838 the reserved lands were ceded to the Indians ". . . to have and to hold the same, together with all the rights, privileges and appropriations thereto belonging to the Cherokee Nation forever." Later, for some Indians, the transition to the property concept was completed when their Oklahoma lands were allotted among the residents and ownership was vested in the individual. Others, like the Navahos, have clung to their concept of communal ownership, and land-use policy is determined in tribal councils. The Navaho's view has always been that natural resources are common property—the coal in the ground, the timber of the mountains. In the eyes of some observers the Indians had a land ethic. We had none. But then came the conservation movement.

FIRST CHALLENGES TO THE COMMODITY CONCEPT

Early challenges to the commodity concept of land came mainly from two schools of thought. There were the first American conservationists with Gifford Pinchot, Theodore Roosevelt, and Major John Wesley Powell outstanding among them. And then—looking at the urban problem—there was Henry George.

George elevated the perception of land from that of a mere factor of production to the central resource of the universe. "On the land," he said, "we are born, from it we live, to it we return again, children of the soil as truly as is the blade of grass or the flower of the field. Take away from man all that belongs to land, and he is but a disembodied spirit."

Land is a free gift of nature, George said, and releases her wealth by man's labor. Individual property in land denies to labor its own product.

Landowners had a right neither to the land itself, he said, nor to the value which social integration adds to the land, nor to the improvements which are inseparable from the land. The user of land was to be entitled to the product of his capital and labor on the land but not to the rent. That was to be taxed away. The value of the land derived from the community and should be returned to the community. In this way, Henry George made a big contribution to ideas about land taxation. He pointed out the sense in which land value derives from two sources: (1) location value, and (2) the value of improvements.

A tax on the location value of land would not destroy incentive as George saw it, but would stimulate production by bringing land held for speculation into use. Population would be dispersed from areas of high density to those where it was sparse. Redistribution of this social income would reduce inequality at the same time that the land tax increased economic growth.

Along with Henry George's effort to express a new view of land as a community resource, there was a growing concern with the lack of planning in urban land use. Men of vision recognized that the overcrowding, ugliness, and disorder of the city could be ameliorated by a proper concern for conservation. Frederick Law Olmsted conceived of a central park in the heart of Manhattan. Unlike the economic man who weighed costs against revenues in the calculus of private investment, Olmsted was a visionary who valued the potential benefits that future generations would inherit. In the mid-nineteenth century he conceived of public gardens, open spaces, and playgrounds to improve the quality of city life. But in city after city the economic imperative overcame the emergence of an urban land ethic.

The urban crisis—mainly a problem of class, race, unemployment, poverty, education, and crime—is also a problem of land use. Our lack of appropriate land-use policies is in part responsible for the present state of affairs. We have brought both suburban sprawl and inner city blight upon ourselves by our lack of vision and our absolutist views of ownership and use of the land.

Edward Banfield argues that both urban sprawl and inner city blight are not new phenomena, and both have resulted from mainly economic factors. In the days of horse drawn carriages people settled close to the source of their livelihood. Local economic growth both drove them from their homes and gave them the means to move. Growth made the commercial value of the downtown properties too high to support residences, and many of the activities in manufacturing and trade made the downtown locations undesirable as residential areas. As the well-off moved away from the changing city, the abandoned neighborhoods were replenished with wave after wave of immigrants. The electric commuter train in 1870, and later the automobile, facilitated the movement of the well-off away from the noise, dirt, and disorder of the city. By 1915 two and one-half million automobiles were in use. The pattern was set. Highways were built to enable commuters to travel from their semirural homes on larger lots than the city had ever afforded them. Manufacturers too sought acreage on which the lower rents would enable them to build more efficient single-level factories.

In this way have the spread suburb and the inner city blight unfolded. Both were caused mainly by the absolutist commodity concept of land. But not everyone has viewed the pattern of urban growth and the commodity concept of land from the benign perspective that Banfield has taken.

While George and Olmsted were mainly concerned with the urban problem of the day, others were preoccupied with even broader visions of conservation. George Perkins Marsh was one of the first to challenge what Stewart Udall has called the American myth of superabundance. In 1864, Marsh argued that the qualities of the land are not indestructible. One of the first to be concerned with the balance of nature, he argued that every part of the animal community had its particular plan in the web of life. He believed that all of man's large-scale engineering projects on the land resulted in unforeseen harm and said, "We are never justified in assuming a force to be insignificant because its measure is unknown, or even because no physical effect can now be traced to it." To disturb the balance of nature without considering all of the consequences was potentially disastrous. Clearly, his arguments carried little weight with early private developers. But they did arouse a response in other conservationists. In 1878 Major John Wesley Powell of the Interior Department laid out a land-use plan for the western United States. In it he called for public irrigation of the western lands with water rights accompanying property rights in irrigable lands. He drew up plans to optimize grazing on the arid soils. However, in Udall's words, "His report used bear language in a bull market, and most of the Western leaders would have none of it."

Other early conservationists were more successful. Gifford Pinchot pioneered in forest management and established the U. S. Forest Service under Theodore Roosevelt. He argued that government planning was necessary to save the forestlands of the west. As in early strip mining, any timber company that stopped to reforest and prevent erosion in the highly competitive logging industry courted bankruptcy. Pinchot argued that the idea of reserving forest lands to remain as untouched wilderness was irrational—in part because western timber men would never tolerate such a policy. Instead he proposed a system of forest management whereby the forests could be used and yet conserved through a rational plan for self-renewal.

From 1871 through 1906 a Commissioner of Fish and Fisheries was created, Yellowstone National Park was established, forestlands were set aside, national wildlife refuges were created, and the work of the Forest Service begun. This conservation movement finally subsided with the coming of World War I, but it re-emerged in the thirties, when dust storms and floods battered impoverished farmers.

In that decade the Soil Conservation Service was formed, the Taylor Grazing Act was passed, and large river valley development projects were launched. Among these was the Tennessee Valley Authority—a land-use planning effort of vast proportions. Soon, however, the conservation movement subsided because of World War II and its preoccupations. Yet it was to surface again in the 1960s with a firmer intellectual foundation, broader public support, and new codewords.

Ecology

Long before economic philosophers were constructing mechanistic models from the borrowed premises of Locke's and Newton's natural law and Bentham's individualistic utilitarianism, practical men were learning about conservation. Deforestation was viewed as a social problem in Europe as early as the thirteenth century. In the late eighteenth century Europeans saw the connection between deforestation and falling supplies of groundwater. The land shortage in the Netherlands started a land reclamation program in the 1800s. Lime and manure for fertilizer were in common use in land-short Europe.

Not everyone believed in the arid and abstract microeconomic notion that nature was only a huge machine and that man could master nature's forces without unforeseen consequences. Visionaries like George Perkins Marsh intuitively understood the systematic characteristic of our living environment. By 1864 Marsh explained the basic ecological concept. Every part of the plant and animal community, from microscopic organisms to earthworms to buds to trees to mammals has its place in the web of life. To destroy any part of the web is to threaten the entire community. Marsh foresaw that draining lakes and marshes and altering rivers by such devices as "channelization" could have unforeseen side effects on water tables, wildlife habitats, vegetative cycles, and the micro-climates.

In *Man and Nature* Marsh said:

> The ravages committed by man subvert the relations and destroy the balance which nature had established . . . ; and she avenges herself upon the intruder by letting loose her destructive energies. . . . When the forest is gone, the great reservoir of moisture stored up in its vegetable mould is evaporated. . . . The well-wooded and humid hills are turned to ridges of dry rock . . . and . . . the whole earth, unless rescued by human art from the physical degradation to which it tends, becomes an assemblage of bald mountains, of barren, turfless hills, and of swampy and malarious plains.

Today the role of land in nature's life cycle is much better understood, but the insights of people like Marsh have been verified. In describing the role of land in the balance of nature Aldo Leopold refers to the "land pyramid" of energy absorption.

Plants absorb energy from the sun. This energy flows up through a pyramid-like circuit called the biota. The bottom layer in the pyramid is the soil; upon this is a plant layer, then an insect layer; another cross section includes rodents and birds; and so on up to the larger carnivores. As we proceed up the pyramid each successive layer of life is less abundant. One plane of interdependence is the food chain. Each species is a link in many dimensions such as soil-corn-cow-farmer. The pyramid is a vast system of similar chains, all interdependent. Food chains conduct energy from the soil up the pyramid. Death and decay return it to the soil.

When a change occurs in one part of this system of circuits, the other parts must adjust. Man imposes rapid and large-scale shocks to which the systems cannot adjust.

In sketching the role of land in the balance of nature, Leopold wished to emphasize three things: (1) Land is not merely soil; (2) native or local plants and animals keep the energy circuit open; others might not; and (3) manmade changes are of a different order than evolutionary changes, and have effects more comprehensive than is intended or foreseen.

Can the alterations we want in the life cycle be accomplished with less violence? Can the systems adapt? In the past some regions have and some have not. In the future, Leopold argues, intelligently planned land-use policies must take these physical relationships into account. But the problem is compounded by the fact that we have only just begun to understand the infinite complexities of the life cycle and land's role in it. The most minute particles in the soil can be critical to its successful maintenance.

Does not this new knowledge of the critical role of land in the balance of nature call into question the concept of land as a mere commodity? Can the market system respond without change to the needs of nature's life cycle? Economic science and real estate law evolved and developed without benefit of this new knowledge. Does this mean that the conclusions of conventional microeconomics and law will lead to perverse results in land use? And can we adapt the calculation of benefits and costs in market transactions to the new knowledge of ecology?

ACTION AND ACTIVISTS

What effect is the new knowledge of land as a resource having on land use? The renewed appreciation for the aesthetic and spiritual value of land has spurred the development of new concepts in land use; proponents have already brought some of them to fruition in the form of improved urban zoning, greenbelts, greenways, and new ways of developing suburban residential properties.

Twenty-eight percent of England and Wales has been set aside for greenbelts and country parks. This action has resulted from passage of the Town and Country Planning Act of 1947, which introduced noncompensable land-use regulations as the main method of guiding urban growth. A 1944 plan established a contiguous greenbelt around London in which private development has been limited. Many of these open-space areas in Great Britain are open to the public although privately owned. Public access is obtained through a consideration paid by the state to the owners.

Similar greenspaces have already been set aside in the United States. A shining example is the Willamette River Greenway in Oregon. The existence of a floodplain turned out to be a fortuitous circumstance for preserving much of the region contiguous to the river in a nearly wilderness state.

In 1966, Karl Onthank, Dean of Students at the University of Oregon, proposed that the areas contiguous to the Willamette in the 120-mile section between Eugene and Portland be set aside as a greenspace. Governor McCall set up a task force to study the proposal, and a comprehensive land-use plan was presented to the legislature.

This project points up the kind of conflict that the new concept of land as a resource must eventually resolve. The first Willamette plan was to acquire private lands along the banks of the river without resorting to eminent domain. But many farmers refused to sell. They had legitimate concerns about access to irrigation waters and about how the public might litter and vandalize their property. Provision for these concerns was eventually made, but it meant redefining the farmer's property rights as the farmers originally understood them. It also pointed up the need for clarification and specification of the scope, boundaries, and characteristics of the greenway plan.

ENVIRONMENTAL ABSOLUTISTS

There are absolutists on either side of the issue, of course. Juxtaposition of extreme views gives us an insight into the attitudes of the absolutist environmentalists—the cutting edge of change in land-use policy. We have already seen how the philosophy of unlimited land development often produced undesirable side effects of erosion, ugliness, and barrenness. Most people viewed these developments with indolent disregard. Others were incensed and driven to action. Among the latter was John Muir.

Muir was enraptured by the wilderness, and he perceived it with a scope and profundity that transcended the intellectual plane of cognition. Udall reports that Muir sought as many contacts with the wilderness as one man could absorb.

> To him, the true wilderness experience was far more than mere exposure to nature; it began with heightened sensibilities and ended in exactness of observation. He felt the same reverence for the land—the sense of wholeness and oneness—that had been experienced by the Indians and the early naturalists.

He became convinced that it was essential to permanently preserve large tracts of choice lands untouched in their wilderness state.

When Muir came to Yosemite Valley, the sheep and sawmills were already there. There had to be a direct confrontation. Notions of a welfare economics *quid pro quo* beneficial to both sides were out of the question. To Muir, the money-changers had to be driven from the temple:

> . . . Through all the wonderful, eventful centuries since Christ's time—and long before that—God has cared for these trees, saved them from drought, disease, avalanches, and a thousand straining, leveling tempests and floods; but he cannot save them from fools—only Uncle Sam can do that.

This driven man was instrumental in setting aside Yosemite National Park and in founding the Sierra Club.

His perspective is critically important in understanding the evaluation of land-use policy; it can best be summed up by quoting his comment on the damming of California's Hetch Hetchy Valley.

These temple destroyers, devotees of ravaging commercialism, seem to have a
perfect contempt for Nature, and, instead of lifting their eyes to the God of
the Mountains, lift them to the Almighty dollar.

Dam Hetch Hetchy! As well dam for waterlands the people's cathedrals and
churches, for no holier temple has ever been consecrated by the heart of man.

The perspective of history thus shows that the roots of today's ecology
movement stretch back at least a century. Even the language of the early
conservation and environment movement is antithetical to that of the developer. In real estate parlance, there is "raw land" to be bought, inven-
toried, and "manufactured" into "improved" land. Then, the land is
marketed with promises of prosperity and happiness: "Your opportunity
to purchase five magnificent acres of America's dwindling real estate."

To be sure, developers are only responding to what the market wants
and can buy. In California, between 50,000 and 100,000 acres of rural land
were subdivided annually in the late sixties and early seventies by recreational lot sellers. It is absurd and unfair to blame developers for supply-
ing what the market demands. Indeed, innovative developers lead the way
in showing how environmental balance can be built into the pricing
structure. The issue of rethinking land-use policy, far from a vendetta
against development, is a search for improved development with a survival value, a search for balance between growth and environment.

THE NEW CONSERVATIONISTS

What are the origins and sources of the effectiveness of the new ecologists? Accompanying the new tools of analysis in the life sciences that have
had such a significant effect on the development vs. conservation issue of
the sixties, are innovations in political action methods and in public relations. Environmental groups, in effect, have learned how to get public
attention and to lobby using methods long familiar to advertisers and to
business legislative organizations, working "within the system."

For example, in the early sixties a proposed dam at Bridge Canyon on
the Colorado River would have backed up a reservoir 18 miles into Grand
Canyon National Park. In early 1964, the Izaak Walton League, at its
conference of more than a thousand conservationists, developed a political
coalition, a general strategy of action, and a public education campaign.
With the help of a hired professional advertising agency, the group placed
a full-page advertisement in the New York *Times*. The National Parks
Association produced an engineering study to show that Bridge Canyon
Dam was not economically feasible and was not needed. By 1965, plans
for the dam fell through.

By 1969, the Citizen's Crusade for Clean Water organized 38 environmental groups to press Congress to increase spending for building waste
treatment facilities. They too were successful. By 1970, environmentalists

were able to generate a nationwide organization, mainly of college students. Students and faculty not only responded with enthusiasm to environmental teach-ins, but through the nationwide attention created by Earth Day began a series of changes, still continuing, in business executive action and in political sensitivity to environmental issues. Meanwhile, the subsequent development of the technique of legal intervention through bringing suits under existing statutory or case law has made environmentalists a powerful force in land-use decision-making.

In the 1970s the waning of enthusiastic, general, and popular support for smokestack prosperity—for the one-dimensional pursuit of a quantitatively rising standard of living—can be seen in the emerging sentiment for slowing population and/or economic growth in particular localities. Examples are given in the 1973 report, "The Uses of Land," by the Rockefeller Brothers Fund.

Coloradoans voted overwhelmingly to bar the use of state and Denver city funds for the 1976 Winter Olympics. In New York State, 70 percent of the voters approved a $1.15 billion bond issue to develop cleaner air and water, solid waste treatment, and the purchase of environmentally sensitive areas. In Florida, voters approved a $240 million bond issue to buy environmentally threatened lands. California voters approved a bill to create state and regional commissions to control coastal development. Boca Raton, Florida, voters set a ceiling on the number of housing units in that city.

Some of this concern smacks of protectionism and exclusiveness. All of it manifests a new concern for the total quality of life.

The Need for Land-use Planning

Modern urban and industrial growth is overwhelming our traditional systems of land management. More than 10,000 governments today regulate how land is to be used, though much land is under no zoning restrictions. The various levels of government cannot, however, function together to solve common problems of land use. Literally scores of federal organizations already have some responsibility over some aspects of land-use management.

Unrestrained and piecemeal spread of urban areas that enshrines growth as good in itself but often ignores social costs has spawned dreary suburbs, neon jungles, strip cities, widespread disregard of the earth's resources, and rising popular discontent.

But no-growth is no solution. No-growth policies of affluent localities are often selfishly inspired, designating development itself as the enemy, favoring the transfer to others of the implacable costs of life itself. The hard fact is that the needs of the U. S. population can only be met by continued development. An estimated 60 million people may be added to the U. S. population by the end of the century, to be housed, fed, and provided with jobs. Between now and the year 2000 we may have to build a new home, school, hospital, or office building for every unit now in existence.

No one should believe, either, that metropolitan growth will lag. Today 95 percent of the U. S. population lives in, or within commuting range of, just 171 urban regions; two-thirds of us live on only 2 percent of the land area. Future population growth could be disconnected from our highly articulated system of urban regions only at enormous expense, if at all. As a result, the whole strategy of isolated "new towns" is open to grave scepticism.

Far from crowding, however, the typical U. S. family yearly uses more and more space. With higher incomes have come higher levels of consumption, more cars, more recreation, more travel, bigger homes, second vacation-homes, and therefore people using more space and spreading farther out over the land. To be sure, by 1985 the household formation rate will grow one-third faster than during the 1960–1970 decade. But, the urban land area is increasing far faster than the urban population or urban households, as American families spread themselves out over a wider range of living space.

Optimists about urban planning, however, ought not to confuse comforting words like *rational,* or *balanced,* or *orderly* with reality itself. Government at all levels is now stuffed full of narrowly defined units or special-purpose units engaged in "planning" land use. What is more, long-standing governmental policy has set land-use planning goals almost inadvertently, such as the depression-born farm policy, the suburbs-spawning FHA, and the Interstate Highway System. Indeed, for years the farm programs took land out of agricultural use while federal reclamation created more. In government, "rational is as rational does" should be the rule.

And in recent years, the conflict over protection versus development led us to cutting off our nose to spite our face. Energy industries, furnishing the basic power to an expanding population, lived through repeated delays in trying to build more supply. In several states—California, Florida, and New York among them—both fossil and nuclear plants were held up. The Alaska pipeline, and offshore drilling in the Gulf of Mexico and the Atlantic Coast, were also delayed year after year. Delaware ruled out refineries on its bayshore coastline.

Everyone wants power but not plants; this paradox of prosperity extends to other industries, and it leads more and more people to the conclusion that we must arrive at a new set of ground rules to meet the demand for improved environmental quality while providing the growth America must have for its future.

Economic growth requires the use of land for mineral development as well as energy supply and use. The luxury of choice does not exist for mineral and energy development; it must occur only where the resources are located. And as our nation becomes more and more energy and mineral deficient, and thus dependent on foreign sources of supply, the value of land for development gets comparatively higher.

THE STATUS OF LAND-USE LAWS

There are plenty of state land-use laws on the books. Ten years ago Hawaii was the only state with land-use controls. By 1973, California, Colorado, Florida, Maine, and Vermont had asserted strong planning authority to directly control their land. Many other states approached land-use planning in other ways.

Hawaii, Vermont, and Maine had zoned all their land, possibly a harbinger of the future. Delaware and California had established strong coastal restrictions—in a country where half the people now live fifty miles or less from some coastal shoreline, including the Great Lakes. Colorado's proposal provided for state intervention in land-use planning when localities fail to act. And states were perking up their ears to the American Law Institute Model Land Development Code—also the federal proposals—to designate environmentally critical areas and regionally significant developments as a way of combining state and local responsibility for land-use planning.

Among the various federal proposals, Senator Jackson (D-Wash.) put forward in 1973 what was called the most far-reaching environmental bill ever considered by the Congress. The bill was short of being a national urban land-use policy; it was really an act to enable states to do planning review, leaving the vast majority of land-use decisions with the local governments.

Under the bill Congress would provide grants-in-aid and technical assistance to the states to help them develop knowledge, institutions, methods, and processes for land-use planning and management. The bill would have a substantial impact on decision-making in four "critical" areas—(1) key facilities, such as airports, major highway interchanges, and the like; (2) large-scale development, on non-federal lands, to be defined by the states; (3) areas of critical environmental concern, such as historic sites, natural hazard lands, renewable resource lands, and the like; and (4) land use and development of regional benefit, such as sewage treatment plant sites, low income housing, etc.

The findings of Congress set forth in the bill are revealing. They acknowledged a national interest in more efficient land-use planning; a lack of recognition of land-use impact of public and private programs; a lack of land-use planning; a lack of consultation with property owners, users, and the public in land-use decisions; a lack of federal agency attention to land-use effects of agency programs; a hindering of significant land development resulting from failure to plan; and a failure of states and local governments to exercise adequately the primary constitutional authority and responsibility they have for land-use planning and management of non-federal land.

The bill would set up a land-use policy administration in the Interior Department and assign to the Secretary of the Interior the responsibility for administering the act. It would set up, as well, an inter-agency board with representatives from the Departments of Agriculture, Commerce, HEW, Transportation, Treasury, The Atomic Energy Commission, The Environmental Protection Agency, The Council on Environmental Quality, The Council of Economic Advisers, and the Office of Management and Budget; plus advisory members drawn from the states (2), localities (2), and regions (1). The federal machinery thus established would have the job of parcelling out the grants to the states as carrots, to get underway effective state-wide land-use planning processes in the first three fiscal years after the bill passed, and to get delivery within five fiscal years state-wide programs of land use. The bill assigned a strong review function to the Secretary of the Interior, and it laid out in some detail the technical requirements for creating an effective process of planning.

The bill, which passed the Senate in 1972, had what one writer called "broad but shallow" support. Despite three years of hearings, the bill heavily emphasized procedures and abounded with loosely defined and ambiguous language, probably representing wise drafting for what nearly every legislator knows in his bones would have interfered with the property rights of homeowners and developers as well as the zoning powers and actions of towns and suburbs. However, legislators also knew that environmental improvement was one of the few policy proposals that attracted voters in the 1972 elections to favor increased spending. Of the 57 candidates for Senate, House, and gubernatorial posts endorsed by the League of Conservation Voters, 43 from 25 states were successful.

No one thought the Jackson bill was going to solve the nation's land-use problems. It really would have just gotten us on a start toward state-wide planning. One criticism of the bill as drafted at hearing time was its lack of balance. One way to get balance is through the principle of compatible multiple uses of land. This principle, employed early in the history of federal land management, could have been effected by setting performance standards for lands. This approach, quite important for example in tidal lands, simply pushes off onto land users the costs of meeting the desired standards, thus internalizing these costs in the price of that land use.

RESOURCES AND PROPERTY RIGHTS

The principle of performance standards for multiple uses of land gets this discussion around to the larger questions of the effect of federal legislation. It would seem that, to be effective, a program of land use should:

—Recognize and maintain the value of the private decision-making process.
—Balance economic and other considerations.
—Provide for compatible uses of lands and waters.
—Put the main burden on states or interstate regions to execute and on the federal government to review and enforce state and regional plans, give financial aid, and balance regional, state, and local needs with the national interest.

These principles, operating together, produce a kind of land-use policy consistent with competitive enterprise and the protection of private property rights in accord with sound environmental, economic, and social values.

There is no doubt, for example, that we as a people have the resources of knowledge that could vastly improve our inventory and our planning methods in land use, if they are applied. What nobody wants is the antiquated and rigid methodology of physical planning to be spread out, at this late date, throughout the states and even between states. This is certainly not the time for a proliferation of the decision-making process of local governments to state levels and on to the federal level.

It is also no time for building a cumbersome framework, called "rational planning" but ending up in adding layer upon layer of narrow and bureaucratic approaches to "impact statements," "enabling provisions," and the like. Once imbedded in the federal judicial process, such legal-planning processes only create developmental sludge, judicial myopia, and red-tape jungles to stifle all but the most ponderous business units.

A lot can be done, legislatively, with brief statements of policy, such as the Employment Act of 1946, compared with compendiums such as some of our taxation and housing legislation. And the reason for wishing the former needs no explaining to the businessman who now has to get 20 permits from as many agencies, or who discovers in mid-passage requirements that spring up like jonquils in early spring.

The Jackson bill was only a beginning of federal interest in land-use planning. Things to come could be explored by a look at the 1973 report, "Land Use and Urban Growth," for the Task Force on Land Use and Urban Growth, chaired by Laurence Rockefeller, of the Citizen's Advisory Committee on Environmental Quality.

The report had strong recommendations on public acquisition of greenspace and preservation of historic sites. But it argued as a concept for tougher restrictions on the use of privately-owned land in order to protect "critical environmental and cultural areas." These restrictions, it believed, have to be upheld by the courts so as to be borne without payment by the government, thus relating the restrictions to the "takings" issue;

that is, the proscription in the Fifth Amendment to the Constitution, ". . . nor shall private property be taken for public use, without just compensation."

The report argued for a new body of environmental law regarding land use, marked by shifting the burden of proof onto proponents of changes in natural ecosystems to demonstrate the nature and extent of the resulting changes. It urged the Supreme Court to reexamine precedents holding for a balancing of public benefit against land value loss. In the protection of natural, cultural, or aesthetic resources, as the report recommended, a mere loss of land value should not justify invalidating the regulation of land use.

In other regards, the report also showed a trend toward reshaping property rights in the development of communities and regions, in terms of greater recognition that land is a natural and community resource subject to depletion, that recreation land is irreplaceable, and that even developmental rights themselves are separable from land ownership and might be separated from it in the way we presently separate mineral rights from land ownership.

OUR OWN DESTINY

In summary, by 1973 land-use legislative and study proposals were moving the United States further toward a national land-use policy that tries to balance environmental protection and economic development. They signified a new public understanding that land is, at least in some respects, an irreplaceable natural and community resource and not merely a commodity for buying and selling. Based on exquisitely patient scientific study, this realization of the "connectedness of life," far from a passing fancy, generates public conviction of great energy and force, not likely to be denied, but if anything to gather momentum, in coming years.

In short, our 300 years of footloose expansion over de Tocqueville's "boundless continent" is effectively at an end. There may be plenty of room out where the deer and the antelope play; but private property will be conditioned in the future by the realization that "This land is your land, this land is my land, from California to the New York Island, from the Redwood Forest to the Gulf Stream waters."

As we try to learn what we do not now know—and that is how to build communities in our great urban regions that are environmentally sound and racially open—we are going to live through a period of great ferment. Conservation alone is not the issue, but neither any longer can sheer economic growth alone maintain supremacy. Both conservation and economic growth must become part of a larger effort. We must learn how to create in our land, communities that we want, that respect the laws of man and nature, and that balance growth and environmental objectives.

For years it has been good enough for developers of both home and business properties to solve the problems of urban facilities for living and working by lavish use of energy both in buildings and in cities, often indifferent to the liquidation of more and more natural features of the landscape. As a business magazine says, "They have taken over the wetlands, filled in the ponds, planed down the hills, put the streams in pipes." And up to recently, to do so has been to give the people of the U. S. the suburban dream house that they wanted.

Now, however, the nation wants something better than mile upon mile of monotonous brick and asphalt, acre on acre of barren suburban landscape, and the substitution of manmade artifact for the plant and animal life that keeps the natural air and water processes in balance. Businessmen are caught in the middle of a great shift in national values that will require new standards of business competence and complex trade-offs that create new definitions of wealth in natural surroundings.

The answer is obvious to state but difficult to attain. It is to develop new framework rules that fully reflect the realism of scientific knowledge about the environment, that assign to it the right priority, and that balance the benefits of freedom and growth against the irreplaceable value of natural processes. The issue of land-use planning is not an issue of "solving problems" but of reexamining and recreating processes of planning in both business and government, processes that reflect and embody both our knowledge of economic growth and our new knowledge of and respect for the environment.

The worst solution would be to recoil from the hitherto unpaid costs of growth to adopt rigid and out-dated physical planning controls. They would lock into the concrete of legalistic haggling all the dynamism of which the enterprise system has been and can continue to be so capable.

Not much better an approach, however, is a response from business itself that would see government drag industry, kicking and screaming, face to face with the realization that our common interest and that of our children's children in survival on earth with decent air to breathe and water to drink does have precedence over the fate of particular methods of energy and mineral development, house-building financing, and property transfer.

Equally bad would be to throw out the baby of private ownership and private competitive enterprise in a burst of intellectual arrogance that attributes the general ignorance of the past, shared by business, government, and consumer, to business itself as the creator of the artifacts of the past. In a society that swims in a sea of new knowledge, what can be more arrogant than to blame the ignorance of the past for leaving undone the tasks of the future?

To the extent that we all accept the premises of science, try to understand them, and adapt new knowledge to our priceless values of freedom and shared knowledge and power, applied always with the restraints of checks, balances, and respect for truth, we have a chance to build together a new republic, even in the third century of this nation.

Perhaps we need to heed still the sad admonition of Chief Sealth of the Duwamish Tribe, who wrote to President Pierce in 1855, in part as follows:

> When the last redman has vanished from the earth, and the memory is only the shadow of a cloud moving across the prairie, these shores and forests will still hold the spirit of my people, for they love this earth as the newborn loves its mother's heartbeat. If we sell you our land, love it as we've loved it. Care for it, as we've cared for it. Hold in your mind the memory of the land, as it is when you take it. And with all your strength, with all your might, and with all your heart—preserve it for your children, and love it as God loves us all. One thing we know—our God is the same. This earth is precious to him. Even the white man cannot be exempt from the common destiny.

The author wishes to acknowledge the generous assistance in research and writing of Dr. Paul A. Reardon, economist, Chamber of Commerce of the United States; with help from an exchange of views with Dr. Arch N. Woodruff, Chancellor, University of Hartford.

A. M. Woodruff

2

Recycling Urban Land

Introduction

THE "IRON LAW"

For better or for worse, cities are among man's most durable artifacts. Their durability means that land, once committed to a particular use, will not be casually or capriciously recycled. An "iron law" determines the process of recycling: property is not recycled until the land under a building is worth more without the building than the combined value of land and building for any purpose to which the building can be put.

An example may clarify the "iron law." Let us assume that a large plot of cleared land would be worth $50.00 per square foot for a major building, but several sub-parcels within the main tract have old buildings on them, rented for enough to justify a combined land and building value of $60.00 a square foot. Recycling under these circumstances is not likely; but if the value of the cleared land rises to $65.00 a square foot, while the capitalized income flow from the improved sub-parcels justifies only $60.00, the whole plot will soon be cleared and re-used. Similarly, if the income flow of the improved parcels drops and justifies only $50.00 a square foot, while the value of the cleared land is $60.00, the plot will soon be cleared. In simple terms: people seldom tear down profitable buildings except to build something still more profitable.

Educator, administrator, urban land economist, and advisor to government, ARCHIBALD M. WOODRUFF *is Chancellor of The University of Hartford. Dr. Woodruff has been Professor of Insurance and Urban Land Studies at The University of Pittsburgh, Vice Chairman of The Allegheny County Planning Commission, Chairman of The National Capitol Planning Commission (1960–62) and Dean of the George Washington University School of Government. He has published extensively in the areas of business, land use, and economics.*

The purpose of this chapter is to comment on the past history of this process, and the factors affecting recycling in contemporary American cities. Relatively uninhibited market forces were involved in most recycling episodes up to about 40 years ago. Recently, government has intervened extensively. This chapter develops, among other things, the argument that government programs designed to follow and encourage pre-existing free market forces tend to be effective, whereas any programs to halt or reverse free market forces must be massive to have appreciable impact, and may well prove to be ineffective. A mild shove will move a stalled car downhill. A strong effort is required to push the same car uphill.

In 1974 most American cities, after a century of volatile development and incessant change, have reached a point where many of the structures in them are obsolete. As a nation, America is impatient with obsolescence and ready to abandon artifacts still useful in favor of others which promise more results with less effort, or which at least have more pushbuttons and chrome trim.

The presumption is general that in the next decade our obsolete cities will be considerably rebuilt. If so, the land will be put to a different use; it will, in other words, be recycled. By the rapidly shifting canons of contemporary good taste, the word "recycle" enjoys wide approbation. It connotes conservation of scarce resources, prudent use of irreplaceable assets, and generally good national housekeeping.

FACTORS AFFECTING RECYCLING

Recycling depends on a series of factors among which the following seem to have special importance.

  a. Locational Stability—Cities are where they are for many different reasons. If the reason remains economically valid, which is to say that if investors think they can still make good money there, then one essential condition is met.
  b. Population Growth—In a growing city investors tend to recycle land, usually in its more congested parts. In a city with a stable population investors have less incentive. If the population is declining, they have small incentive.
  c. Growth of Affluence—If numerous individuals are growing richer, even if poverty is also present, there will be persons interested in recycling. If people, especially influential people, are growing poorer as during the American depression of the early 1930s, few investors are likely to recycle land.
  d. Technology of Construction—Any major change in the technology of construction encourages new building to take advantage of whatever is new. If the change also permits more money to be made, recycling forces are correspondingly strengthened.
  e. Transportation Systems—Changes in the urban transportation system affect investor decisions. Systems (and private cars on highways are a "system") tend to (1) concentrate people and hence business more intensively

in an already established area of concentration, or (2) in a new area or areas, or (3) conversely reduce concentration and scatter economic activity.

f. Urban Geography and the Metropolitan Patchwork—Modern metropolitan areas in America sprawl across the jurisdictional lines of the independent units of local government. Marked differences in the level of local taxes, or local service, can drastically affect the disposition of public and private agencies to recycle land in one community rather than another. The resulting jurisdictional patchwork enables some communities to create a favorable climate for recycling while others seem to be displaying hostility toward fresh investment.

g. Availability of Land—If the land is available at reasonable cost, investors are more likely to foresee profits. Land may become available when (1) ground leases on a large tract expire, (2) some large owner decides to sell, or (3) several owners of contiguous property agree to sell simultaneously. If land is not available at prices which investors consider reasonable, new investment is improbable. Land may be unavailable because (1) it has been divided into a large number of quite small plots, too costly to assemble; or (2) the expectations of land holders (that is the prices at which they will sell) are higher than the profit expectations of developers (that is the prices they feel they can pay for new investment).

h. Investor Expectations—The foregoing seven factors influence what investors think they can pay. If equity investors foresee profits, and mortgage investors agree with them, new developments are highly probable. Otherwise new development depends on government underwriting.

i. Government Involvement—Government is involved negatively and positively. Zoning laws may be, and frequently are consciously intended to be, barriers to new development. Local tax concessions may be and often are meant to be stimulants. The state governments participate in the tax concession game. The federal government and the state governments participate in other activities, chiefly through outright subsidies and laws making the power of eminent domain available to assemble sites.

j. Disaster—Historically much recycling has followed upon disaster, natural or military, which wiped out large urban areas. Much of Rome was rebuilt after the fire which occurred in the reign of Nero, with or without musical accompaniment. Much of central London was rebuilt after the fire of 1666; St. Paul's Cathedral and several other memorable buildings date from this disaster. Cologne was largely destroyed during World War II, as was Coventry, England, and both were rebuilt. In America disastrous fires in many cities, Boston, Chicago, San Francisco, and several others, cleared large areas which were then comprehensively rebuilt. Since disasters of this sort occur only unpredictably and every effort is made to prevent them, this factor is mentioned only in passing.

THE LONG HISTORY OF RECYCLING

The long history of urban land recycling merits more than a casual backward glance. Episodes of recycling have been triggered by key events such as the conversion of a city to a local or national capital, or the establishment of some major institution. The same trigger effect can be produced by a change in the transportation system, such as a new bridge, or tunnel, or a new rail or a highway line.

Throughout the world and over the centuries, most urban land *has* been recycled, some of it innumerable times. Archeologists excavating the site of Homeric Troy, starting with Schliemann in 1871, found nine successive cities, one on top of the other. Troy was recycled vertically from prehistoric times until fairly recently. Rome and many other cities of long history and stable location have also been recycled vertically.

Cities have always been luxuriant producers of waste products, although never before on the magnificent scale of modern America. The problem of waste disposal goes back as far as mankind's written records, and one of the common practices has been to throw the waste out the back door, and when it gets conveniently deep, to build something on top of the midden. The process was never quite that simple, but archeologists constantly find evidence of cities rising vertically on top of their own potsherds.

A certain amount of vertical recycling took place in the United States in the nineteenth century. As a young appraiser in the 1930s and 1940s, the present writer often found in the basement of a building the remains of the foundations of previous buildings.

One alternative is horizontal relocation. This is standard practice among nomads and semi-nomads. Once a campsite is polluted and the readily available firewood consumed, the populace moves.

While recycling was common and probably "normal" among cities of stable location, history also records examples of cities which, instead of being recycled, were totally abandoned. Cities were abandoned in Asia; and Inca cities like Machu Picchu were abandoned in South America for reasons about which we can now only speculate. Abandonment seems to have occurred much less often than recycling.

The cities of the industrialized west had two recent episodes of especially active recycling. The first occurred in the nineteenth century when, in a very short span of years, the technique of erecting tall buildings with elevators, central heat, and electric light was developed just at the moment that the trolley car was revolutionizing urban transportation and concentrating economic activity downtown to a hitherto undreamed extent. The second occurred when the trolley was superseded by the auto, which tended to scatter what had previously been concentrated; and this period coincided with a considerably changed approach to the construction of factories.

Factors Affecting Recycling

LOCATIONAL STABILITY

The factors which influence land recycling in a city start with the reasons for the city's location. Some cities have been "permanent," waxing and waning to be sure, but remaining in the same place literally for thousands of years. Other cities have been, if not "permanent," at least locationally "durable"; still others are transitory. Investors will recycle land in a transitory community only if they can make a fast profit. Typical real estate investments involve long commitments, and mortgage financing is obtainable only if the lender has a firm expectation that the area and the specific location within will prosper throughout the life of the mortgage.

A mining town is an example of a transitory community. Towns have to be established where the ore body happens to be, and they tend to wither as soon as the body is mined out. The American West has its full share of such towns with romantic names and legends of barroom brawls. Towns which are tied to transportation systems have sometimes been "durable" and sometimes "permanent." The very early (pre-Jewish) dwellers in Palestine were, according to some archeological evidence, caravaneers, driving donkey trains between Damascus and northern Egypt. The donkeys, who needed service stations about every seven miles, were overtaken by technological obsolescence when the caravaneers domesticated the camel. The camel had a broader range, and required less service, so the smaller caravansaries tended to wither and the larger ones to prosper. A related phenomenon occurred in the American West. Many towns existed as farm markets, about as far apart as a man could travel in a day with a horse and wagon. When the auto superseded the horse, these towns declined, while a small number of larger trading centers prospered. During the heyday of steam, railroads built water tanks and other service facilities quite close together. The diesel did to the water tank what the camel did to the donkey caravansary. The "tank towns" generally tended to wither. Towns like this were "durable." Their survival depended on outside factors which seemed unlikely to change, but which did change with drastic consequences to the towns.

Capital cities, national or regional, tend to be permanent, as do cities which grow up with or around major institutions. Rome, Mecca, and Jerusalem are permanent; St. Peter's, the Kaaba, and the Wailing Wall are unlikely candidates for early relocation. Princeton, New Jersey, and Rochester, Minnesota, are permanent for like reasons. State and national capitals tend to be permanent because so much money is tied up in monumental architecture.

Many major cities are located where well-established land routes and water routes intersect. The "silk road" stretched across Asia before the dawn of history; where it reached the Mediterranean Sea, it met water routes of equal antiquity. Cities flourished in this area before Solomon reigned in all his glory, or even Minos who had still more glory but a less effective press corps. Really safe harbors have always been rare, and those which combine a cozy anchorage with easy defense are even rarer. Men picked these locations before they learned to write, and their descendants live there still.

Syracuse, New York, is a good modern example of a city at the inter- section of important routes. Two centuries ago major footpaths east and west crossed equally important north/south trails. One hundred fifty years ago, the Erie Canal intersected with a major north/south canal. One hundred years ago, and until recently, the east/west rail lines crossed major north/south lines. Now Route 90 east/west crosses Route 81 north/south, from Washington, D. C. to Montreal.

Large settlements generally are more permanent than small ones. They are more apt to have a diversified economic base, and size has its own drawing power. During the middle of the twentieth century the large American metropolitan areas tended to grow and the smaller ones barely to hold their own, while smaller communities outside the metropolitan areas tended to shrink.

POPULATION GROWTH

Most American cities grew rapidly during the nineteenth century and the first quarter of the twentieth. Between 1850 and 1900 the 25 cities which were the largest in 1970 grew seven-fold from 1.7 to 11.2 million. Thereafter, while numbers were larger, the growth rate was lower. Until the 1930 depression, most of the growth was within the boundaries of the cities. Also, especially before 1900, many cities expanded by annexation of surrounding territory. Most American cities, including all the large ones, were locationally stable; and all were growing rich. These factors com- bined to encourage the recycling of downtown land to more profitable uses.

Population continued to grow after World War II, and trends which had been suggested earlier were now dominant; the independent suburbs began to grow faster than the cities. The metropolitan areas which include the 25 cities mentioned above grew three-fold in the 70 years between 1900 and 1970, adding 20,000,000 more people. Whereas the earlier growth had been in the cities, the later growth was mostly in the suburbs; and the suburbs were mostly politically independent. The economic consequences of this political fact can hardly be overstated.

The example of St. Louis offers food for thought. About 1870, the smart citizens engineered an amendment to the state constitution completely separating the city from the poverty-stricken countryside around it, thus reducing city taxes. One hundred years later economic conditions had ex- actly reversed themselves; the county was rich and the city poor. An effort to turn back the hands of time was ineffective. It required a state-wide vote and drew very few ballots except from the immediate area. The county turned down the reunion five to one, because it would have increased county taxes; and the city turned it down three to two, primarily it is felt because the urban inhabitants feared a loss of political power if they were absorbed into a larger whole.

Between 1960 and 1970, twelve of the largest cities *lost* population, while the suburbs of the 25 cities *gained* 24 percent. In the first three years of the 1970s, the central cities collectively lost about 4,000,000 people. Of these about 3,000,000 moved to suburbs identified as part of the metropolitan areas, and an additional 1,000,000 to outer suburbs, just outside the metropolitan areas.

GROWTH OF AFFLUENCE

By any set standards America grew rich in the last century and a half, remaining pockets of poverty notwithstanding. Average per capita income rose from about $1,500 in 1950 to $3,900 in 1970; even discounting inflation, this was a noticeable gain. Affluence reports must be read side by side with population statistics. Before the depression of the 1930s the cities were generally gaining wealth faster than their suburbs, and real poverty dwelt in the countryside. The combination of growing population and rising affluence encouraged recycling in the cities.

The tide turned sharply in the 1950s and ran even more strongly in the 1960s, as the middle class moved out of the cities into the suburbs, being replaced by large groups of the relatively impoverished. In the last 25 years, the stable to declining population of the cities and their relatively declining wealth, coinciding with the growing population and increasing wealth in the suburbs, discouraged further recycling in the cities and greatly encouraged it in the suburbs. The suburbs were where the action was.

TECHNOLOGY OF CONSTRUCTION

Residential—Construction technology was static through most of history; but even so, communities which were growing richer or more populous or both recycled land. Small structures were pulled down and larger ones built, even though the larger ones had only marginally more amenity. The Palazzi of Florence offered little more comfort than the homes of modest burghers, but they were larger and gaudier and did things for the owners' egos. No matter how little extra comfort a big structure provides, someone is always ready to build the biggest house in town. Veblen called it conspicuous consumption.

The technology of house building changed remarkably little from the earliest development of fire-baked brick down to relatively modern times. Six stories was about the height limit, because to go higher required walls so thick at the bottom that they used too much of the ground floor. Spacing of the walls depended on structural timbering and the need for interior light. Candles were expensive and not very effective, so not much work could be done far from a window.

The Romans had both plumbing and central heating, and these amenities survived long in Byzantium, although for centuries they disappeared from western Europe. Monarchs and peasants alike huddled before open fires; and while the better class tailors learned to make handsome fur robes for their exclusive clientele, even the rich and powerful lived in conditions that a middle-class Roman would have considered unfastidious grandeur. Versailles was an example; hordes of servants, lacking sanitary facilities, performed on stairs and in hallways acts now considered uncouth unless performed in seclusion. The resultant odors, graphically described by contemporaries, led to a demand for perfume reflecting a degree of olfactory sophistication on the part of even the most unwashed aristocrat.

The technology of residential construction underwent significant changes during the last three centuries in America, and involved the rediscovery of conveniences common in the better Roman villas. An abundance of building material in America encouraged innovation, especially the use of planks which had been in short supply in England due to labor restrictions. An abundance of land and an independence of character bordering on cantankerousness encouraged the detached single family house. The log cabin, incidentally, was a late comer to the American architectural scene; it did not appear until Swedish settlers arrived on Tinicum Island near Philadelphia.

One major technological change was the introduction of the iron stove. It required only about one-tenth the fuel of an open fireplace, and provided better heat. With stove heat, architects could raise ceiling heights and increase window size. Houses built to the new mode were more comfortable and looked different; and the well-to-do moved to the outskirts where they could buy or build a new house with the "new look." Older houses provided shelter for the newly arrived, a process which began in the seventeenth century and has never stopped.

Other significant changes were the rediscovery of indoor plumbing and central heat. President John Adams reportedly bathed in the Potomac River and on one occasion, it is alleged, had his clothes stolen the while. Andrew Jackson was probably the first president to enjoy anything like a modern bathroom.

Central heat and indoor plumbing were conveniences which were much desired by those who could afford them. The same was true in sequence of gaslight, electricity, and airconditioning. Continuous technological improvements led to a national passion for the new and different, and a national aversion to the obsolete. It combined a taste for luxury with an understandable human desire to demonstrate the ability to pay for it. American families, for many reasons, have been more willing to move to new housing than most Europeans; the rapidly evolving technology of residential construction, and the desire for something new, were part of it.

Office Buildings and Apartment Houses—A fairly abrupt change occurred in the middle of the nineteenth century in the technology of erecting large structures. The eighteenth century "counting house" rose about

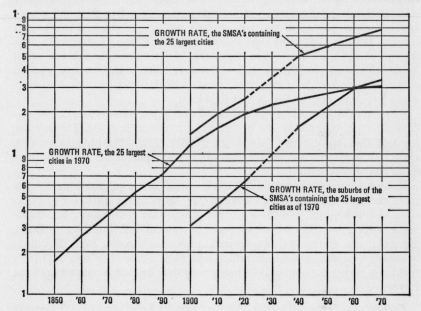

Fig. 1

six stories and usually on a fairly narrow lot. A new day dawned when the Crystal Palace was opened in London's Hyde Park in 1851, the first large iron-frame building. The very next year Elisha Otis demonstrated an elevator. It was operated by steam and it worked after a fashion, and not without hazard; but it foretold things to come. About 1900 wrought iron gave way to steel, and elevators were improved with hydraulic and eventually electric power. Gaslight displaced candles and whale oil lamps, and electric illumination followed. One by one the obstacles in the way of constructing larger and taller buildings were eliminated, just about the time other incentives began to encourage their construction.

A great downtown building boom began as America emerged from the depression of 1873, and from then on the majority of new downtown buildings were steel-frame structures. Architects cautiously added height until 20 stories became common. The Woolworth building reached 57 stories in 1912, and by 1970 buildings of over 100 stories had been built in several cities. The ability to make more intensive use of scarce land by piling stories on top of each other created an incentive to pull down small buildings and replace them with large ones.

What could be done with office buildings could also be done with apartment houses. The idea of large apartment houses was hardly new; the Romans had them, and the English cities which grew in the early industrial revolution produced jam-packed tenements. The idea of luxury apartments was new, as was the idea of building them to considerable heights. Between 1900 and 1930 many large, steel-framed apartment buildings went up, and introduced a pattern of living which enabled much higher densities per square mile than ever before with no sacrifice of comfort. New York's Manhattan Island is dominated by such buildings as are large parts of the Bronx and Brooklyn.

After World War II, a great deal of new apartment construction was "garden type," relatively low buildings in park-like settings. The pre-war concept that apartments were commercially acceptable only in or very close to the downtown area evaporated, and apartments were built in quite remote suburbs.

Recent apartment construction has involved many refinements, but few basic changes. Tall buildings have grown taller, airconditioning has become common-place, and luxurious buildings have grown more luxurious. Some zoning laws have been changed to permit one building to house garage space, offices and apartments, plus some stores. Such buildings become airconditioned cities under one roof. Since they are, relatively speaking, rather economical of energy they may be part of the wave of the future.

Factory Buildings—During the last third of the nineteenth century much of the American industry was housed in multi-story "mill-type" buildings. Highly congested cities like New York had tall "industrial loft buildings." These buildings had their disadvantages, especially the "mill-types." They had masonry bearing walls, and heavy wood interior framing; and the floors seldom could carry more than 80 pounds per square foot with a minimum amount of vibration. Movement of merchandise on elevators was an added inconvenience.

Around the time of the civil war, steam-powered mills began to replace the water-powered operations that had preceded them, and locational considerations changed. Water-powered mills had to be located where stream flow and topography permitted, and company towns grew up around these mills. Steam-powered mills could be located inside cities where the labor force could come to work by trolley car. This was a very great change, its magnitude now obscured by the passage of time. The word "steam" in those days packed the same emotional wallop that the word "electronic" does now.

American industrial technology continued to change dynamically. One major development was the electric motor which freed factories from the belts, pulleys, and shafts by which power had been transmitted from the boiler room to the individual machine. In addition to providing flexibility of lay-out, the elimination of the power belts removed a major industrial hazard. The accidents which happened when arms and legs got tangled in these belts were the stuff of which nightmares were made.

At the same time process machinery got larger and heavier, and much of it vibrated more. Small tractors were developed which moved merchandise around one-story plants more cheaply than it could be moved on the elevators of old multi-story buildings. By World War II the lay-out generally considered optimum was the flat one-story plant; but this called for far more land.

Another American innovation was the well-paid industrial employee who could afford a private automobile. Factories which had once needed to be near trolley lines, now found that they needed parking lots instead. Furthermore, the trailer truck quickly superseded rail as the hauler of Class I freight, and highway access became a factor.

The need for room for one-story plants, parking lots, expansion space, and green grass to look at instead of the in-town locations, forced factories to seek the outer suburbs. Added considerations were highways on which trucks could come and go without knocking over fire hydrants along congested narrow streets and the tax benefits which accompanied a move out of town. Factories could not get enough land in the cities, the suburbs often offered special tax concessions, and all things combined to encourage relocation. By the 1960s most American industry had relocated outside the city limits.

The quirks of urban evolution brought into the cities the migrants of the 1950s and 1960s. The children of the industrial workers of the 1920s were now well established suburbanites with a preference for white-collar employment, while the migrants were lodged in the housing that had once accommodated the factory workers of that earlier period. The factories needed blue-collar workers, the migrants needed jobs; but the jobs and a considerable potential labor force were located in different parts of the metropolitan areas, rather remote from each other and without the link of public transportation.

Energy and Urban Evolution—The last two episodes of rapid urban land recycling coincided with major changes in construction and transportation. Minor changes in both occur constantly, but no major change has occurred until the arrival of what may well be a genuine energy crisis. If the crisis is real and long continued, large detached houses exposed to the wind on all four sides may become so expensive to heat that apartment house living may be preferable. Heavy masonry walls conserve solar heat, and clusters of tall buildings raise the ambient temperature as much as 10° above the suburban level. This happens both in winter when it is desirable and in summer when it is not. Depending on local climate, it may prove to be considerably more economical to heat living space in large buildings in winter and cool it in summer in the north than anything that can be accomplished in single houses. In the south the climate may have a reverse effect.

American urban transportation for two decades has depended increasingly on the private automobile. An individual with access to a car seldom wants to travel in any other way. Possibly gasoline prices will rise so high, or gasoline will become so hard to obtain, that our whole way of life will have to change back from dispersed suburban living to clustered urban living. If this should happen, a third major episode of urban land recycling could be upon us.

TRANSPORTATION SYSTEMS

The Impact of the Trolley Car—The development of the steel-frame building offered a money-making potential unmatched in previous urban history. It opened entirely new vistas to investors both in offices and apartments. This technological development would, by itself, have set off a wave of recycling of urban land from less dense to more dense (and hence more profitable) use. It so befell that it was superimposed on another major change, a genuine revolution in transportation.

People had walked wherever they had to go for so long that the human mind cannot comprehend that much time, perhaps 100,000 years. During the course of this period men domesticated many animals, and a fortunate few rode them or in carts pulled by them, but the percentage of Romans who had private chariots in 74 B.C. was probably not much larger than the percentage of Americans who have private airplanes in 1974 A.D. People mostly walked. The race obviously built up a monumental aversion to walking, judging by the eagerness with which it has abandoned the practice whenever it could.

During the "age of feet" cities developed convenient market squares where housewives could buy their daily bread without walking all day to do it. Medieval Paris had a series of subsidiary squares located in different parts of the city, and retail trade was considerably dispersed. The kind of business concentration that characterized "downtown" in the 1920s simply did not exist; modern business like the modern city is the child of rapid transportation.

About the time of the Crystal Palace, the steam railroads were coming hesitantly of age, and steamships were giving the first challenge to the clipper ships. At the same time, street railways were appearing in American cities, first with horse cars, and then in the 1880s and 1890s with the electric trolley. The electric trolley changed the pattern of human movements in the twinkling of an eye. No longer was it desirable to have houses clustered tightly. The iron stove had removed an architectural limitation on window size, ceiling height, and room size; just so, the trolley removed a space limitation on the placing of structures. American cities which had grown for centuries in concentric rings shifted overnight to a spider web pattern following the car lines.

The trolley car era came quickly and went quickly, lasting at the most a scant century, but it left a major mark on succeeding generations. It foreshadowed the wider dispersion which the auto engendered. More significantly, it provided a sharp focus to downtown which the auto has considerably dimmed, but not quite eliminated. One logical outgrowth was the department store; small store merchandising followed the people during the age when people had to walk. When the trolley made downtown the one spot equally accessible to all metropolitan locations, merchandising began to concentrate there. Obviously, larger stores could carry larger selections, and they became an attraction themselves. Office buildings had to be downtown, because nowhere else could the large numbers of employees be recruited. As the downtown area became more and more concentrated, land values went up and up. Areas of old housing around the edge of downtown became potential sites for new tall buildings and the owners' expectations soared accordingly.

Conversely, the trolley allowed the well-to-do to move out to new sections where builders were providing residences with all the modern conveniences. The immigrants arriving from Europe in large numbers took over the erstwhile residences of the well-to-do together with block after block of new tenements. Much land was recycled into denser and hence more profitable use.

The Counter-Impact of the Automobile—The auto city which followed the trolley car city involved a basic return to the pattern of the foot city which had preceded it. Automobiles and feet can go anywhere a path or road permits; the trolley is bound to tracks. Hence the auto city, like the foot city, sprawled indiscriminately with no particular focus except that inherited from the trolley car. Like the trolley, the auto wiped the miles off the map, and distance which had been a factor in the foot city was forgotten. In about 20 years the auto destroyed the monopoly which downtown had enjoyed in the trolley car era, just as other events were making the city less and less attractive to investors seeking a way to make a profit out of recycling land. To a very real extent the automobile turned the city inside out.

The legacy of the auto to the middle 1970s is a series of metropolitan regions so widely and so randomly scattered as to defy the best brains of the generation trying to contrive a workable mass transit system. The effect on land has been a relative decline in urban land values, a considerable relative rise in suburban values, a tendency for suburban land to be recycled up toward denser uses, and a counter tendency for urban land to stagnate and drift downward to less dense uses. Through all this, the expectations of urban landowners have remained high, and they have been reluctant to release land at prices which investors found attractive to new projects.

The energy crisis may change, may in fact already have changed, our transportation thinking. It has been said in Detroit and elsewhere that Americans would willingly see their civilization perish before they would relinquish their private cars. But perhaps the decision is not to be made in America, but in parts of the world with no affection for Americans and their automotive foibles. If so, perhaps America might find itself again using energy-saving mass transit instead of the energy profligate private auto. And if this happened, the locational focus might reverse itself, the investors' profit equations yield different results, and downtown might regain economic favor.

URBAN GEOGRAPHY AND THE METROPOLITAN PATCHWORK

The American Metropolitan Patchwork—Between 1875 and 1930, when much urban land was recycled, the forces directing investment decisions were fairly straight-forward. Population was growing, citizens were getting richer, builders could erect tall structures, and a changed transportation system endowed downtown with an ever sharper economic focus.

Between 1945, when construction resumed after the depression and the war, and the present, much more land has been recycled; but it has been largely in the suburbs. The forces influencing investment decisions pulled and hauled in various directions. Dynamic new growth generally favored the suburbs; and population movements within metropolitan areas were swift and volatile. Social factors which had been absent, especially from northern cities, suddenly became entangled with political factors which assumed dimensions of importance when urban growth went sprawling across jurisdictional lines.

The governmental structure of the American metropolis has no present parallel in the world and none in history. No other nation, primitive or advanced, has ever expected geographically small units of government, woven tightly together in an economic network, separately to provide such major public services as public education. Most suburbs have more in common with each other than they collectively have with the core city, although some older suburbs blend indistinguishably with the city rather than with the newer suburbs. The city as the site of the oldest settlement became the location for many services which have traditionally enjoyed exemption from property taxes, such as government buildings, hospitals and the like. These are often used by the population of the whole area, but the cost of supporting services to the exempt properties is borne by the city alone.

Until about 1930, many cities grew by annexing territory on their borders. Local government is organized differently in different parts of the country; and some cities were, and still are, surrounded by township or county land. Many states allow cities to annex such land, but prohibit the annexation of land from incorporated boroughs, villages, or towns. The varying nomenclature tends to obscure a simple issue. Cities generally could absorb only unincorporated areas; and as time went on and people living outside the city limits wanted more urban-type service like sewage disposal, more and more areas were incorporated. In due time many cities were surrounded by independent incorporated units, and horizontal urban growth depended on voluntary consolidation. The nation's most conspicuous example was New York, but there were many others. Noteworthy recent consolidations have involved Miami, Jacksonville, Indianapolis, and Toronto. However, the separate suburbs mostly cherished their separateness and fiercely guarded their jurisdictional ramparts. After World War II, consolidations have been few and far between.

The result is a series of geographically small independent units of local government, each of which can levy taxes only within its own borders; but each of which must render the whole panoply of public services from police protection to public education. Rich towns can do it easily; middle income towns can do it with some difficulty; and poor towns can do it barely, if at all. The tax rate reflects the degree of effort; it is highest where the town is poorest. And in the early 1970s the poorest communities are the smaller of the old central cities.

Tax Differentials—The differentials are considerable. Effective rates in central cities are often twice the average of the city's suburbs. The effective rate is what the rate would be if property in each community were assessed at 100 percent of market value.

The impact of a local tax differential is blunted because an investor can offset his local tax against the income which will be taxed by the federal government. Partly for this reason and partly because of investor inertia, most small differentials in local taxes seem to have minimal influence on investment patterns.

This is not true of large differentials. The high taxes usually associated with central cities are "over-capitalized"; and, relatively speaking, the lower suburban taxes are under-capitalized. That is, an investor with a jaundiced eye on high city taxes might assume that these tax dollars represented forgone income that would have been capitalized at 12.5 percent, whereas his roseate view of the suburbs suggests that their lower taxes should be capitalized at 10 percent. Differentially high taxes are never an isolated phenomenon. Other factors raise or depress investor expectations, but these factors usually tend in the same direction as the tax differential, and the various factors aggravate each other.

Social and Economic Movements within Metropolitan Areas—During the 1960s a large number of black people left the cotton fields of the old south to seek their fortunes in northern and western cities. The black population of the south was almost static during the decade of the 60s, but the black population of New England increased by 37.3 percent, of the Middle Atlantic States by 29.5 percent and the Far Western States by 36.4 percent. The migrants sought better jobs, a more pleasant social environment and better welfare provisions. Connecticut, for instance, paid as much welfare per week as Mississippi paid per month. A somewhat similar wave of Mexican-Americans poured into the cities of the southwest. Toward the end of the decade a considerable number of Puerto Ricans came to New York and New England.

Mayors and councils responded by increasing educational and welfare budgets; and few, if any, of them foresaw the whole dimensions of the problem. The source of funds was the local tax, chiefly the property tax; and just so much could be done with this resource. Unfortunately, the more they did, the more attractive the cities became to fresh migrants; and the numbers increased. The presence of migrants discouraged the older and more well-to-do residents, who increasingly moved to the suburbs. The cities raised their tax rates to meet rising costs, and this encouraged more working taxpayers to leave. The whole grim combination reduced assets just as costs were rising. The cities too late realized that they were in the position of the overzealous cubscout trying to rescue the drowning giant; the spirit was willing, but the capability was inadequate. The poverty of the migrating groups was a national problem; no city could solve it single-handedly, and coordination of effort was scandalously lacking.

The migrants, black, Puerto Rican or Chicano, had suffered social repression; and, denied access to the channels of law enforcement which were taken for granted in most cities, they had a tradition of settling their arguments on the spot by direct, ungentle means. Their children, with a heritage of near-illiteracy, reacted differently to schooling than did the children of people who had for generations had the advantage of excellent schools. The proclivity to direct action and the educational difficulties induced many white families, especially those with children in school, to leave in near-panic and establish new homes in the suburbs. Thus the migration into the metropolitan areas was matched by another one within the areas, almost always across town lines. Once established in the suburbs, the new residents pushed for zoning and building laws to exclude all but the well-to-do. As their numbers swelled, so did the effectiveness of their voice in the legislatures, where the suburbs tended to oppose tax systems which would shift any significant part of the cost of ameliorative social programs away from the cities.

Balkanized Zones of Poverty—The cities increasingly became balkanized zones of poverty, while the suburbs became equally balkanized zones of affluence. For example, in 1970 the average income of a Hartford, Connecticut, family was $9,995, while the corresponding figure for the Hartford suburbs was $14,843. Affluent black families went suburban just like white families, the average black suburban family income being over 1.6 times the corresponding figure for the city.

Housing inventory figures for metropolitan areas (SMSA's) affirm the decline in central city housing. The cities between 1960 and 1970 added 4.2 million units and lost 2.8 through demolition, for a net addition of 1.4 million. By contrast, the suburbs added 7.7 million units, and lost only 1.5 million, for a net addition of 6.2 million.

These stark figures tell part of the story. Merchants can, up to a point, lure customers from considerable distances; but only up to a point. Then some competitor moves his store closer to the customers. As the higher income groups moved to the suburbs, the large stores tended to follow them. In 1948, 71.4 percent of all department store sales were in the downtown headquarters and just a little more than a quarter in the suburban branches. A decade later the suburbs had captured a generous third, and by 1972 a generous half. Department store sales increased considerably in 1973 over 1972, and the growth rate in the suburbs was well over 10 percentage points higher. For example, in Buffalo, New York, and Washington, D. C., the suburbs grew 15 percent, while the city had no gain. Another measure of declining urban economic vitality was the urban mortgage delinquency rate; a recent study in the Pittsburgh, Pennsylvania, area indicated that the "trouble" rate was 47 percent lower in the county of Allegheny outside Pittsburgh than in the city.

Low-rent housing in the cities became more and more densely crowded; and as occupancy exceeded design capacity, deterioration accelerated. Housing codes were next to impossible to enforce, once the buildings were saturated with people; the people could be evicted, but they had, in fact, no better place to go. The suburbs got their housing laws passed before the migration engulfed them, and, by starting early, they found they could enforce density laws. Evictees simply moved back to the city. Within the cities considerable rent came from the welfare departments, and they maintained at least minimal housing standards for their clients. When these were violated, the welfare department tended to move clients to borderline "good" housing which seldom stood up well under the numeri-

Fig. 2. Population and Family Income in Central City and Suburbs—

> *Bridgeport, Hartford, and New Haven—*
> *Black and Other—*
> *1970*

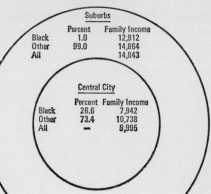

HARTFORD S.M.S.A.

Suburbs

	Percent	Family Income
Black	1.0	12,912
Other	99.0	14,864
All		14,843

Central City

	Percent	Family Income
Black	26.6	7,942
Other	73.4	10,738
All	—	9,995

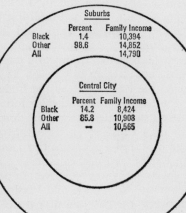

BRIDGEPORT S.M.S.A.

Suburbs

	Percent	Family Income
Black	1.4	10,394
Other	98.6	14,852
All		14,790

Central City

	Percent	Family Income
Black	14.2	8,424
Other	85.8	10,908
All	—	10,565

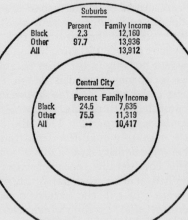

NEW HAVEN S.M.S.A.

Suburbs

	Percent	Family Income
Black	2.3	12,160
Other	97.7	13,936
All		13,912

Central City

	Percent	Family Income
Black	24.5	7,635
Other	75.5	11,319
All	—	10,417

cal impact. The added pressure depreciated the urban housing stock and further induced the middle class to move out.

Property Abandonment—The combination of factors produced in the late 1960s and early 1970s a phenomenon seldom hitherto observed, namely the large-scale abandonment of property. A property is abandoned when an owner ceases to pay taxes, and ceases either to occupy or to try to collect rent. This movement involved some stores, some factories, and many tenement houses. It reached epidemic proportions in the early 1970s. New York City is probably the world's largest owner of urban property.

Abandonment is clearly associated with unprofitability; owners who have any expectation of profit do not abandon. The suggestion has been made that abandonment has been heaviest in cities with rent control, but statistics are lacking either to prove or disprove this contention.

American municipal government, noted neither for forethought nor planning, has seldom reacted less decisively to a problem than it has to abandonment. Crumbling buildings are simply left to crumble. Laws empowering the cities to establish title and demolish structures are grossly inadequate, but few cities have sought legislative clarification. The cities need to seize these properties aggressively, demolish most of them, and then keep the vacant lots clear of junk. If cities fail to do so, the derelict buildings are occupied off and on by the sub-welfare stratum of humanity, drifters on the edge of the law, prostitutes, dope handlers, and other criminals who cherish anonymity and are willing to suffer the resultant discomforts. The crime rate in such structures is high. As Sternlieb and Burchell say in *Residential Abandonment*:

> In Newark, of all index crimes taking place within the city, nearly 4 percent now take place within abandoned buildings. In this city, ten murders, fifteen rapes, and close to 150 incidents of assault and battery occurred in 1971 within vacant buildings. For lesser crimes, the same year saw close to 200 incidents of malicious mischief or disorderly conduct violations, and 100 incidents of narcotics offenses. Finally police assistance was required for at least 23 natural deaths and close to 50 cases of falls, animal bites, sickness and the like.

No city can long afford many abandoned structures. The land under them could be converted into a recyclable asset, but only through energetic municipal action.

Experience in Other Countries—The experience of other countries has not coincided with that of America. Many countries, if not most, have experienced a major migration of the impoverished from the countryside to the cities. The migration has been most pronounced in Asia and South America, and less pronounced in Europe. With relatively few exceptions the newly arrived poor have clustered around the outside of the city, and some of the clusters have become squatter colonies that must be seen to be believed. Relatively few affluent people have decamped; mostly, they have remained happily enjoying the urban advantages of small houses or apartments reasonably close to the thick of things. Many factors have played a part in the contrast between this country and urban areas elsewhere:

1. Americans have more autos and use them more, hence are more mobile.
2. Americans have had a taste for one-family house living; apartment living dominates in Europe and Asia, and much of South America.
3. Well-to-do Americans have not enjoyed having their children in the same schools as the children of the very poor, because of different behavioral patterns and learning patterns. Europeans and Asians react the same way, but have generally found other ways to accommodate popular wishes without segregation by municipal boundary. Virtually all other countries have national or state-operated schools rather than locally operated ones.
4. The tax systems in other countries seldom differentiate significantly among portions of metropolitan regions, whereas the differentiation in America is very great.

Some cities have been substantially rebuilt in the last quarter century with a major improvement in housing for the disadvantaged. Hong Kong and Singapore are especially good examples, but many others could be named. For all their undiminished rhetoric, few communist countries have matched words with deeds. The city of Moscow is a conspicuous exception, with a very substantial production of housing for low and moderate income families.

Danger lies in over-generalization; but to accept this hazard, it appears that American cities in the 1970s had a three-fold disadvantage compared with cities elsewhere: (1) auto transportation had turned them inside out, making the suburbs highly accessible to those who could afford them; (2) the balkanization among parts of the metropolitan areas had isolated the poor in politically separate enclaves, mostly in the urban cores; and (3) the local tax system greatly aggravated points 1 and 2.

AVAILABILITY OF LAND

Land is always available at a price. The price may be low enough to attract investors despite other factors which would discourage them; or it may be high enough to prevent investment in the face of other factors which might encourage it. The price which owners ask depends on their expectations of future values. The price which developers and investors offer depends in turn on *their* expectations; under present American income tax laws, capital gains become an especially important objective of their strategy. When the expectations of owners and developers are at substantial variance, property can stay stagnant for considerable periods of time.

An additional constraint limits the availability of urban land. The older parts of many cities were laid out in very small lots, and a would-be investor must purchase several to get enough land to build a large new building.

The Process of Open Market Assemblage—In order to get enough land, many developers of the 1870s and 80s became assemblers. Seeing the investment possibilities inherent in the new large structures, they bought up clusters of the little "original" lots until they had enough land, perhaps 40,000 square feet, to build a tall steel-frame building. Some lots in the old cities of the northeast were as small as 16 x 60; many were 18 x 80 or 20 x 80; and 25 or more would be required for a 40,000 square foot assemblage.

In the 1870s and 80s owners, conditioned by long continued trade in small lots, were attuned to the values generated under six-story buildings. The developers, seeing the future, were willing to pay more than the "old" owners thought of asking, and trade was brisk. The "old" owners speedily learned the rules of the new game, and the process of land assemblage henceforth became one of the world's most fascinating sports when played among contestants of near equal ability.

The actual process involved making unobtrusive and carefully camouflaged offers to owners, using a series of intermediaries to conceal the identity of the actual assembler. He might use dozens of agents and record titles in many different "straw" names. His devout hope was to bamboozle the public and especially the "old" owners, until he had control of the parcels he needed.

Despite all efforts at concealment, word very often leaked out; and when it did, the owners who had not already sold jacked up their prices. The assembler expected this and tried to get the early purchases in hand at the lowest possible figures in order to leave himself room to overpay for the last few and still keep the average square foot cost within his limits. This meant that the lambs that came early to the shearing got shorn to the quick.

Other assemblers were always eager to enter the game. Many had spies in the courthouses to keep an eye on any suspicious cluster of deeds all recorded in a short time. The assemblers used every device available to avoid disclosure, unrecorded deeds, contracts of sale, options, and bonds for deed, depending on the custom of the particular state. Once a rival assembler caught wind of an assemblage, his obvious ploy was to try to buy into it, that is to persuade the owner of a key parcel to sell to *him* rather than to the first assembler. Then the rival sat back and awaited a call from the first assembler. Properly handled, this could produce a small fortune for the rival; and as professionals at the game, they usually outplayed the amateurs.

Time was money in this game. Assemblers tied up capital, even though they tried to defer closing and actual taking of title as long as they could. The assembler had to pay taxes, interest on borrowed money, and forego interest on any of his own money that he used. A smart assembler managed to use very little of his own money; it was too easy to use other people's. Property under assemblage usually paid some rent, but seldom enough to be an attractive investment for its own sake. Hence a stalled assemblage was to be avoided.

Some assemblers started two or three projects simultaneously, using one or two as smoke screens for the other. Sometimes a developer, stalled by a hold-out, built a large building around two or three sides of a small one. They derived a special satisfaction from leaving a rival assembler thus painted into a corner. The surrounded building lost all of its nuisance value as soon as the developer went ahead, and most of its value for any purpose. The writer knows of one hold-out who refused $150,000 in 1892, and got "built around." His grandson sold to the owner of the surrounding property in 1948 for $60,000; considering interim inflation this was about one-sixteenth as much as his grandfather had refused. Grandpa had suffered from greed and bad timing.

A frequent player in the assemblage was the "spoiler." His ploy was to buy key parcels in many different blocks where he thought assemblers might operate. He did not hold these in his own name, but in "straw" names hopefully suggestive of unsophisticated little old ladies. The spoiler won handsomely if an assembler fell into the trap and tried to put together a plot including his spoiler parcel. His ultimate killing came if the assembler got the whole plot together except *his* piece and then went broke. The spoiler then stepped in and bought up the assembled property for a song. With a little luck (good for him and bad for his rival) he could turn a profit of 1000/1.

The spoiler lost if he bought at the wrong times and the wrong places, and wound up with a string of bad properties which no assembler wanted. The writer appraised in 1954 such a string of dead spoilers, which a wealthy man had acquired 30 years before.

Open market assemblage was a game played without mercy for very high stakes, and only the nimble-footed and level-headed survived. The opportunities for fortune were obviously greatest when the owners of small parcels had a limited economic horizon, whereas the assemblers saw larger vistas. It was a thrilling spectator sport while it lasted, but it took a heavy toll of the players; and when transportation systems began to favor the suburbs over the central city, many developers turned their eyes in suburban directions. Profit expectations had shifted enough so that both they and the mortgage lenders felt that the odds favored such ventures as shopping centers and outlying apartment projects.

The remaining projects within the cities were very largely office buildings plus a few hotels. Developers continued to assemble urban land, but the process was slower paced than it had been in the frenetic 1920s. Most purchases were made when a developer could buy at a price he liked, which would provide an adequate if unexciting return in case he had to hold on for a considerable period. Acquisition of key parcels still involved high pressure dickering, but the pressure was considerably below the 1920s level, because so much of the development energy had been drained off into the suburbs.

New office buildings were built in large quantity in New York, Washington, D. C., and several other cities, where the demand for such space remained high. They were technologically similar to the buildings of the 1920s except for far more exterior glass, and universal airconditioning. Many of them replaced older office structures. Some, in Washington, D. C., for example, replaced blocks of old residences. Downtown merchandising decreased between 1945 and the present, and aside from non-profit ventures like the Kennedy Center in Washington and Lincoln Center in New York, recreational structures were rare. Downtown increasingly became a specialized office headquarters.

Assemblage, An Example—An example may elucidate what the previous section painted with a broad brush. Let us assume a modest 20-story building to be erected on a plot 100 x 150. The building would have 300,000 square feet of space, and in 1969 would have cost about $20 per square foot of $6,000,000. On completion it would have yielded gross rent of about $2,000,000 at an annual operating cost including taxes of about $1,200,000. The net of $800,000, capitalized at 8 percent, would indicate a value of $10,000,000. By deduction the land would have a residual value of $4,000,000 *after the building was completed.*

The developer in 1969 could have obtained a loan of 75 percent at 6 percent for 25 years. The debt service would be about $500,000 and the owner's equity return about $300,000. In 1969 he would have wanted 12 percent on equity and this figure sets the limit on his land purchase at $2,500,000. The difference between land cost and land residual is his cushion against the unforeseen; and if the building is completed as estimated, it is his entrepreneurial profit.

Let us assume further that he needs to buy 9 parcels to complete his assemblage, and that he has already bought 8 of them. He bought 3 for $200,000 each, 2 for $225,000, when the word began to leak out, and then 3 respectively at $250,000, $275,000 and $300,000. So far he has fleeced the lambs in a fashion he finds satisfactory, and he has now run into another assembler who has "bought in on him" and holds the ninth and key parcel. He can, if he has to, go just over $600,000 for this last parcel, and his rate of equity return obviously goes down as this purchase goes up. Somewhere around $600,000 he is in enough trouble that he has seriously to consider selling out what he already has and dropping the deal. If he sells, he can make a modest profit but nothing compared to the stakes he is playing for. His rival, holding the key parcel, can do exactly the same arithmetic and knows about where the breaking point is. Each developer is a professional, finely attuned to interpret every indication of nervousness on the part of his opponent, down to the last anti-acid digestive tablet. Ulcers flower handsomely as this game is played.

INVESTOR EXPECTATIONS

Investor expectation is frequently expressed in the terms of the length of time required to "get the bait back." A "quick in–quick out" investment is one thing; a long-term holding is another. A developer would be willing to build an office building almost anywhere provided he could lease three-fourths of it to a corporation of AAA national standing, and thus guarantee his costs and a meagre return. He would gamble that he could rent the balance of the space for enough to make a handsome profit. He would be willing to build a store almost anywhere, provided he could lease it to an AAA national chain merchandiser. Assuming the impossibility of either, the developer would be willing to build in a speculative location, provided he thought he could recover his equity money within three or four years at a profit of 20 percent.

The average investor is the ultimate realist. He has relatively little interest in making the city attractive for the sake of making it attractive, or making it beautiful for the sake of aesthetics. If he is old enough and successful enough, he may have reached the point where he likes to build monuments to himself. If, however, he conforms to the general average, his interest is making money. In recent years the average investor has had low expectations of rising land values and eventual profit through the further concentration of economic activity in central cities. He has, on the contrary, had expectation of recurrent losses from the dispersion of economic activity. On the other hand, he expects rising profits from the increasingly active development in the suburbs. Therefore, his long-run expectations induce him to accept a lower rate of annual return on the suburban development than on an in-town development. Table 1 represents an attempt to summarize the forces which influence urban land recycling, the effect they have on investor expectation, and hence on investment performance.

GOVERNMENT INVOLVEMENT

Reason for Government Involvement—The first hints of a major redirection of economic activity came as development resumed after the end of World War II. Within a few years the change was quite apparent to all who chose to look, as developers and mortgage lenders bargained with the

TABLE 1. INDUCEMENTS TO RE-CYCLE LAND IN VARIOUS PARTS OF METROPOLITAN DISTRICTS

	Central City	Suburbs
1. Locational stability	Good.	Good.
2. Population*	Declining during 1960s especially the later years.	Increasing ever since World War II at an increasing rate.
3. Affluence*	Declining in the 1960s and early 70s.	Consistently increasing.
4. Construction technology	Stable. More subject to obsolete statutes and restrictive labor rules than the suburbs.	Stable. Less subject to obsolete statutes and labor restrictions than central cities.
5. Transportation technology*	Favored suburbs during the 1960s and early 70s. Possible reversal due to energy crisis in late 70s.	Favored by auto system since the 1940s. Consequence of gasoline shortage still to be determined.
6. Local taxes	Very high and rising. Many cities now twice as high as suburban average. High taxes encourage business and middle class residents to leave.	Usually a very favorable ratio with city taxes, but suburban taxes have been rising at a rapid rate. Tax advantages remain entirely with the suburbs.
7. Availability of land	Land hard to assemble at prices allowing yields as good as those obtainable in the suburbs.	Land harder to get than a few years ago; but the advantages are all with the suburbs.
8. Investor expectation	Generally bearish.	Generally bullish.

* The energy shortage or what is perceived to be such, has coincided with a period of very high interest rates and a shortage of mortgage money. If the energy shortage is of long duration, economic activity could be considerably redirected, improving the competitive position of the central cities in the matter of population, affluence, and ease of access. A significant change in these factors could change the nature of investor expectations.

major merchandising chains who had long been the largest rent payers in the major urban centers. The stores were unquestionably "going suburban," paying proportionately more for space in suburban shopping centers and proportionately less for what had been prime "100 percent district" space in the core city. They were also willing to make longer-term leases in the shopping centers and tended to hold their urban leases to shorter terms. Sensing the consequences of this economic redirection, groups in various cities began to call for public programs to "revitalize" downtown.

The Pittsburgh Story—Pittsburgh, Pennsylvania, was a bellwether. Its manifest unloveliness had aroused the concern of a remarkable group of loyal Pittsburghers, led by Mr. R. K. Mellon, who had a few years previously asked Frank Lloyd Wright what to do about it. For a substantial fee, Mr. Wright summarized his opinion in three words: "Tear it down." Being a man of large imagination with resources to match, Mr. Mellon sought other solutions and set in motion the forces which led to the establishment of an unlikely but firm coalition of staunchly Republican business leadership with Democratic, labor-leaning Mayor David Lawrence. The combination was unbeatable.

In response to its urging the Pennsylvania legislature allowed the Pittsburgh Redevelopment Authority to use the power of eminent domain to assemble land for urban recycling. Once assembled, the land was to be sold to developers. The first major project was "The Point" undertaken by Equitable Life and involving a cluster of office buildings and a hotel on the site of a former industrial slum. The next project enabled Jones & Laughlin greatly to expand its steel mill within city limits; and several other projects followed. The first few projects were large and were almost unanimously applauded for their contribution to urban aesthetics on the one hand and the tax base on the other. Later projects incurred opposition from displaced residents. The relative success of redevelopment in Pittsburgh may be traceable to the size of the projects relative to the size of the city, and the fact that they began early. Smaller projects in other cities have sometimes turned out to be expensively ineffective. Pittsburgh had 16 federal projects with expenditures to mid-1972 of about $120,000,-000, plus the "Point" and Jones & Laughlin projects which involved about $250,000,000 more in state and private money. This came to $700 per capita, a very high level by national standards.

Federal Program of Urban Redevelopment—The federal programs, Pittsburgh included, date from 1949. The first law stated in its preamble that its purpose was (1) to revitalize cities and strengthen their tax base and (2) to clear slums.

Local redevelopment authorities were to propose projects in blighted areas. The proposals were screened in Washington for the award of grants to permit detailed planning. The plans were then meticulously reviewed, and if approved, funded in large part with federal money, initially two-thirds–one-third and later three-quarters–one-quarter. The local contribution was usually in the form of the value ascribed to parks, streets, school sites, fire and police stations, and in-place infrastructure. The procedure changed in detail from time to time, but remained essentially unchanged during the quarter century of urban renewel. To mid-1972, about 450 projects had been approved and $6.25 billion expended out of allocations of $10.5 billion. The remaining $4 billion plus presumably will be spent as projects reach completion.

The largest beneficiary has been New York City with $346 million; next is Philadelphia with $308 million. Only 31 percent of the total federal funds disbursed went to the largest 25 cities. One very large recipient per capita was New Haven at $1,000.82.

Projects were supposed to be located only in blighted neighborhoods. Standard housing was defined, and housing which failed to meet standards was *ipso facto* blighted. Standard housing required central heating, plumbing inside each apartment, a window in each bedroom, reasonably good overall conditions, and an absence of overcrowding. Determination of blight was left to local planning commissions, and such criteria as "reasonably good condition" were sufficiently judgmental that what was deemed blighted in one city might not be invariably so judged in another.

The program of urban redevelopment was impeded by the high cost of land. The expectations of urban landowners remained high, and many people, including local governments, looked for an early return of the "good old days" when the downtown district was the clearly established center of regional economic activity. In litigated land acquisition cases the rules of evidence tended to emphasize optimistic estimates of land value, and to withhold such contrary facts as property abandonment. Testimony stressed "highest and best use." The former owners who had abandoned property obviously thought that no one would soon come forward to make such use of the land; the owners who held out to the point of litigation displayed a better sense of timing, through business astuteness, political foreknowledge, or sheer good luck. Non-litigated cases generally followed the guidelines of the court holdings, and the overall pattern was one of high acquisition cost.

The story of land acquisition for urban renewal has another side. Like the old commercial assemblers, negotiators for the renewal authorities tended to make low starting bids, hoping to acquire the first batch of properties inexpensively to leave room for subsequent dealings. Some owners, through eagerness, ignorance, misdirected good citizenship, or equally misdirected trust in the negotiator as a government representative, accepted the first offer and wound up in worse shape than needed. Many could not find new housing or relocate a small business with the amount realized from such a sale.

In summary, the land acquisition system worked badly; weak and gullible owners were undercompensated, obdurate owners were paid too much, and the high land cost discouraged urban recycling. Land cost led Congress to introduce another subsidy in the form of a write-down on the land. A redevelopment authority could sell land to a developer for less than cost, the consideration being based on the income expectation of the new project.

Did Urban Renewal Clear Slums?—The answer is negative, although the program helped more than it hurt. Very few slums in all history have been "cleared"; many have been moved. Unsanitary buildings can be destroyed, but the people who occupied them rarely did so from choice; poor people live in poor and crowded housing because they are poor and it is inexpensive. When such housing is destroyed in one location, the occupants perforce find another. Human poverty is not a problem of recent origin; nor is it a problem for which a solution has ever been found.

Part of the logic of urban renewal was that once the very worst housing was destroyed, those displaced would find other housing slightly better, and escalate the general social weal. Early in the program, before the black migration had had an impact on northern cities, this process worked after a fashion, although not without trauma. Two early projects, one in Boston and one in Pittsburgh, involved stable old neighborhoods, ethnically homogeneous, and with deep locational roots. In the Polish section cleared for Jones & Laughlin, many houses lacked amenities associated with "standard" housing; and most had outhouses. But the section was immaculate and its people were proud. The evacuation was painful, even though practically all of those displaced wound up in "standard" housing. Much the same pattern was repeated in an Italian section of Boston. Housing style was upgraded, and the unwilling beneficiaries were not happy about it.

Later in the program predominantly black neighborhoods were redeveloped, and new factors emerged. In the early 1950s many black neighborhoods were just as stable and "turf conscious" as Polish and Italian sections. But whereas most white refugees had friends or relatives already living in the suburbs, the black refugees did not, and in the early 1950s many suburbs took pains to make themselves inhospitable. Hence the horizontal spreading which followed the redevelopment of a sub-standard white neighborhood did not follow when the same process was applied to a black neighborhood. Instead, the refugees had to shoe-horn themselves into other sections of the city. At the best they were not, in the early 1950s, worse off after the move than before, save for the pain of disruption. But things were just about to get worse.

By the late 1950s the poverty population had over-saturated the housing available in many a northern city. The suburbs had long since slammed the door; now they piled furniture against it. Most efforts to introduce public housing outside the core city were met with refusal on the part of the suburbs. Time became a major factor; most redevelopment projects took five years or more from condemnation and clearance until the new structures were ready. Even if bad old housing was replaced with far more commodious new housing, five years was a long time to wait. The coincidence of three major forces: demolition of *any* housing, no matter how bad, the closed door policy of the suburbs, and the continuing migration into the cities produced a veritable urban witch's brew. The situation was similar to what would happen to a subway train during rush hour, in a station jam-packed with people scrambling to get aboard, if somebody decided to remove a car or two from the train.

The first response was a requirement in the law that new housing had to be found for every displaced family. Considerable effort went into this and even some success, but the urban crowding went on and on. A second response was to concentrate more and more on housing replacement, until eventually this tended to overshadow the rest of the program. Old housing was to be destroyed only if new housing were provided, but even this made the situation temporarily worse because of the time lag between the start of demolition and the completion of replacement facilities. The combination of the migration and the closed suburb had, temporarily at least, produced a dead-end.

Urban population declined in 12 of the 25 largest cities between 1950 and 1960; and with the sole exception of New York, all continued to decline between 1960 and 1970. New York gained about 1.5 percent in the latter decade, but three more cities struck a downturn: Milwaukee, New Orleans, and Seattle. The relative declines in urban population eased the urban crowding, but not to the point where vocal minority groups would stand by with equanimity while poor housing was destroyed to make way for non-housing uses.

Did Urban Renewal Significantly Improve Urban Finances?—No clear answer is possible. To the extent that urban renewal replaced slum property with new un-subsidized structure, housing or otherwise, its effect was obviously positive. To the extent that it replaced dilapidated old housing with subsidized projects, the social effect was probably decidedly good and the long-run fiscal effect poor. Most of the 25 largest cities showed some improvement in the size of their "grand list" (total value of assessed property) between 1960 and 1970, the average growth being about 15 percent; but some cities which spent the most per capita on urban renewal reaped disproportionately small harvest. Newark, New Jersey, and New Haven, Connecticut, were among the top per capita spenders for urban renewal; and each lost heavily on "grand list" between 1960 and 1970. The presumption is that had they not engaged in urban renewal, things would have been still worse.

In most areas the suburban grand lists were growing much faster, and in many cases twice as fast as the urban lists. Effective tax rates rose much faster in the cities; the politically independent suburbs, without the costs generated by a poverty population, enjoyed a bonanza in the form of an immigration of the well-to-do. The taxes on upper middle-class homes pay the education bills for those who live in them, or at least contribute heavily. The shopping centers and the industrial property in the outer suburbs generate tax income very much in excess of any municipal costs attributable to them. Generally the fiscal position of the suburbs improved during the decade of the 1960s and into the early 70s albeit not quite so fast as the fiscal condition of the cities declined.

The hope of revitalizing cities through urban renewal lay in capitalizing on their central location and existing transportation systems, mostly cars on highways, to attract profitable uses which would generate more tax revenue than expenditure. Office building clusters were obvious candidates. The urban renewal projects of the late 1960s, however, tended to replace housing with housing. This had a reverse spiral effect. The urban housing was mostly subsidized, some of it very heavily subsidized. Its occupants were mostly poor, highly fecund, and in need of tax-supported services. Such property generated municipal cost but very little municipal revenue. Hence, far from strengthening the urban tax base, the program tended to weaken it. Furthermore, it committed urban land for a long period, half a century perhaps, to housing the low income segment of the population, and by so doing effectively barred those uses which previously had made the central city "downtown." It planted poverty even more firmly in the city and encouraged the middle class to leave.

Urban redevelopment, being strongly dedicated to the removal of extremely poor housing, tended to start with demolition, and then when the tract had been cleared proceed to wonder what to do with it. From a purely economic standpoint, better results would have accrued from the opposite approach, that is selecting a site and a use designed to rejuvenate urban economic life, and then proceeding with demolition. In practice the two objectives of revitalization and slum removal proved to be less compatible than anticipated.

Other Government Assisted Programs to "Revitalize Downtown"— Either coupled with the use of eminent domain to facilitate assemblage, or otherwise, several cities adopted tax concession schemes to attract investors. Since the local property tax could be locally manipulated and, while not legally immune to outside scrutiny was not much subject to it, various concessions had long been made, especially in communities heavily dominated by a self-perpetuating political group. After World War II various concessions were legalized. One type permitted a government instrumentality to buy land, arrange a lease to a use, frequently a factory, and even issue tax-exempt bonds to cover the cost of the new building. This device was used in many outlying areas to attract factories. Another device was to peg property taxes in the city at some specially low level, either the *status quo ante,* i.e., what the property paid before the new development, or in terms of a percentage of the gross income of the new project. The Prudential Tower in Boston is an example of a large development, the construction of which, long contemplated, awaited legislation permitting the city to make a contract with the developer concerning future taxes. Most commercial development in downtown Boston since then has been under some form of tax freeze. The same is true in several other cities.

Any form of tax freeze establishes a two-tier tax structure and eventually a two-tier rental market. The "grandfather" buildings which antedate the freeze are fully taxed, whereas the new buildings are not. Hence, the new buildings in addition to offering their newness can sometimes offer rents as much as $1.00 per square foot per year less than the old ones. Tax freeze legislation was taken through test cases to the supreme courts of several states by cautious developers. The implications of the two-tier market were not fully foreseen, and this legislation may be challenged in federal court. If overturned, an old set of obstacles to the profitable use of urban land will be resurrected.

An entirely unrelated type of effort to attract middle-class crowds back into the city was the spate of building municipal pleasure domes. Some were dedicated to high culture like the Kennedy Center in Washington, others to more popular recreation such as sporting events. Houston's Astrodome was just one of dozens of municipal centers and arenas, designed to provide large capacity facilities for conventions and sports events. Such arenas automatically become white elephants unless they are heavily used; and this, in turn, has led some conservative businessmen into the odd posture of subsidizing sporting teams, an activity somewhat remote from the financial experience of many of them. The record of such ventures indicates the possibility of small profits and large losses. Convention business carries with it the extra virtue of hotel and restaurant activity.

Some Questions Remaining to Be Asked

WHO GAINS OR LOSES IF DOWNTOWN IS OR IS NOT REVITALIZED?

The largest recent losers, on paper or in cash, have been the owners of fringe downtown property, warehouses, old office buildings and old housing. They had expected eventual profit from recycling their land when investors were ready to build great new towers; when downtown development declined after World War II, their hopes lost substance. Owners who had bought cheaply enough lost mostly hope; some who had bought for higher prices in speculative anticipation lost cash along with their hopes. Furthermore, as taxes rose, some were squeezed between rising costs and static or falling rent. Urban renewal programs to date have helped some such owners, encouraged others, and left still others stranded higher than before.

These events provoked a two-tiered tax structure in some cities. Land under a tall office building is obviously valuable. Nearby land for which no immediate demand exists may be worth very little except to a speculator willing to await eventual development. Contiguous parcels, one developed and the other not, have traded in recent years at startlingly different prices, and are often assessed at startlingly different levels.

The immediate gainers from most downtown renewal projects have been owners of second-class downtown real estate. The losses from urban decline are widely shared. Owners of first-class downtown real estate and surviving homeowners face certain loss as increasingly expensive munici-

pal services are financed out of taxes imposed on a progressively narrowing tax base. Owners who flee face certain loss on the sale of urban property. Large property owners, when they flee from a situation grown un-
bearable, are subject to a degree of contumely not visited upon retreating
homeowners.

MUST THERE BE A CONCENTRATED DOWNTOWN?

A curious nostalgia persists concerning "downtown." It *was* the center
and within living memory practically all major cities had well-defined
centers. The fact remains that, during much of history, cities were not so
sharply focused; and some modern cities seem to have developed without
any centers. Los Angeles has long been described as a cluster of suburbs
without a city, and this description, supposedly mildly humorous but not
entirely inaccurate, has by no means inhibited its growth. St. Louis a century ago had a well-defined downtown along the river; it moved slowly
inland half a century ago, and finally disintegrated. Greater St. Louis is
now a very much scattered community, retaining its overall vitality; but
old downtown is the woebegone relic of departed glory. Perpetuating
downtown because there used to be downtown is a bit like perpetuating
memorial horse-troughs because there used to be horses. Relatively little
evidence suggests that a metropolitan area *has to have* a sharply focused
downtown.

CAN "REVITALIZATION" SOLVE THE URBAN TAX PROBLEM?

No municipalities have actually gone bankrupt since the 1930s, although
many are well advanced on a path that shows no other destination. The
level of municipal service has clearly declined in many cities; in most
cities ameliorative services to the poor have not kept pace with need. The
new urban poor received virtually no such service when they lived in tiny
scattered southern hamlets, so they are not losing anything they had traditionally had. On the other hand, society's collective conscience calls for
major improvements in housing, health, and education. Present evidence
suggests that these cannot much longer be financed from local property
taxes. Following this logic, the services will have to be curtailed unless the
states or the federal government assume a large part of the cost. The addition of new subsidized housing in the urban center aggravates the problem; it dedicates the area to continued occupancy by the needy poor, and
it perpetuates a land use that is exempt from local taxes, with only partial
restitution via "in lieu" payments from the federal government.

A combination of tax-assisted urban renewal with free market investment redirected by the energy crisis *might* improve the urban fiscal out-
look through a new construction boom. It might even improve it significantly, but the numbers are discouraging. Urban tax rates are about

double the suburban average; Hartford, Connecticut, is not untypical of geographically small northern cities which have gone beyond the limit of their own fiscal capability trying to provide services needed by the newly arrived poor. Hartford's tax rate is an effective 5.5 percent compared with about 2.5 percent in those suburbs where investors can also build. Noting that the profit expectation is high in the suburbs and low in the city, it would take more than rebalancing the tax load between the city and the suburbs to get investors excited about urban possibilities. Just to re-balance the tax load, Hartford would have to *double* its tax base. The base is now about $1 billion of assessed value or about $1.6 billion market value. Hence, Hartford would have to add $1.6 billion of new construction without adding a cent to municipal costs, just to get equal with its own suburbs. This is hardly a realistic expectation. Such a volume of new construction is hardly to be anticipated in the whole state of Connecticut in the next five years, and the experience of the recent past has been that the bulk of new construction sought the lower taxes and greater profit expectations of the suburbs.

SHOULD WE CONSIDER LAND BANKS AND LEASE-HOLDS?

One prerequisite to the recycling of urban land is the availability of tracts large enough to permit profitable re-use. Urban renewal has been at the very best a much qualified success. Lacking acceptable quantitative measures, the results must be evaluated on the basis of judgment. Gener-ally, the cities which spent fairly heavily per capita got fairly good results, with the exception of Newark, New Jersey, which was a heavy spender, but an all-around loser. A few cities, fortuitously located with respect to the overall population drift from east to west, prospered with zero renewal expenditures or with very small ones. Generally, the cities that sought large results from small expenditures in redirecting their internal econo-mies were disappointed. If this suggests any one thing, it suggests that renewal projects have to be large to be effective; and to be large, a great deal of land is needed.

This tentative conclusion, rather widely but by no means unanimously shared by urban economists, suggests two courses of action, neither of which is inconsistent with the other. The first is land banking. This is the acquisition of land by government whenever and, within reason, wherever possible, in advance of any designated need for the particular area, and holding it until ready for use. The obvious objection is that politics in-evitably intrude in such public actions, at least in America, and valuable rights, publicly controlled, tend to be alienated to private profit in mo-ments of relaxed public vigilance, or sometimes in the face of contrived emergencies.

The second method is that of handling all public property by lease-hold rather than by free-hold. That is, if a city acquired a large tract for urban renewal, or for land banking, it would *never* sell the property in fee, but would lease it for long terms, such as 50 years, to developers who would have that much time to get in and get out. At the end of 50 years the tract would revert to the public intact and could be recycled.

The Australians have had considerable experience with lease-holds. The city of Canberra is basically a lease-hold community. A Commission has recently considered this matter and has concluded that suburban land being developed should be on lease-hold for the precise reasons just given; after an appropriate period large tracts would revert to the government for re-use, obviating the painful process of assembly either in the open market or through eminent domain. The city of Stockholm is another very good example of leased land.

Since most of the value of land is the result of things the government does, an eminent domain acquisition compensates an interim landowner for benefits conferred upon him by government. For well over a century, various social philosophers have questioned why society should create value and then buy it back from private holders.

In addition to the foregoing, Australian cities had in them large tracts which a century or so ago were granted by the Crown to churches or race tracks. Much of this land was leased to private parties who built on it what the Australians call terrace houses. At the end of the leases, the tracts reverted, and large blocks of land were available for redevelopment. Very few similar occurrences have taken place in America.

The United States, however, is by no means unacquainted with lease-hold procedures. The whole western grazing area is dotted with government leases to ranchers. Within the last quarter century urban lease-holds have been created in many cities for complex financial reasons not germane to this subject. Experience in lease-hold administration has been accumulating in this country as well as in Australia.

SHOULD WE CONSIDER THE CITY WITH THE "HOLLOW CORE"?

The free market forces seem to be producing the doughnut city. Good new development, unless strongly motivated by artificial means, has been going into the suburbs, convenient to middle-class residents. The central city has become more and more isolated. Large owners of commercial property, faced with unhappy choices in a few cities, first employed additional guards and maintained fortresses in the midst of urban disorder. Employees could drive into guarded compounds and stay there until the end of the day. When this type of procedure became more of a nuisance than the company could tolerate, it moved all or most of its activities into a "safe" suburb where its employees could come and go without undue trepidation. Something like this has happened in a few American cities. Another example is the construction of Makati outside of Manila in the Philippines, a new "downtown" built on the outskirts.

Two factors encourage the development of the doughnut city. The first is the widespread construction of ring highways. The prototype is Route 128 around Boston. A location along Route 128 has somewhat the same general accessibility that downtown once had. Every suburb can get at it, and fairly quickly. Boston established a tax concession and a massive program of urban redevelopment, and these brought new buildings to downtown. Should a federal constitutional case disturb the tax concessions on the new buildings or should their taxes for any reason skyrocket out of reason, then a sub-center along Route 128 might easily supersede old downtown.

A second factor, also technological, is far better telecommunication. One standard reason for the existence of downtown is that business people need to be close to each other in order to transact business. Television screens attached to telephones are a present reality; so is the instant transmission of documents by wire. These two make it possible for business meetings to be conducted "face to face" although the persons involved may be blocks apart, or miles, or continents.

The doughnut city is a real possibility; but not a nice one. An impoverished population, understandably restless, will not remain passively in the hole of the doughnut. Nothing in history suggests that such a population can be forcibly held down, and nothing suggests that the collective conscience of the nation feels they should be. The lesson of history is, in fact, that they must be lifted up until they share most of the advantages enjoyed by the great middle class.

CAN THE ECONOMIC ATTRACTIVENESS OF THE CITY BE REESTABLISHED BY OTHER MEANS?

The economic disincentives to investment in the central city are an amalgam of insalubrious social conditions and high taxes. The former discourage middle class white people from coming downtown when they do not have to. The latter speak for themselves; disproportionately high urban taxes coupled with inferior municipal services constitute a tangible disincentive. The tax situation *could* be remedied by any of several events, or a combination of them, unrelated to the recycling of urban land.

If the State Assumes Educational Costs—Much current litigation is pending along the lines of the California case, *Serrano v. Priest,* in which the state Supreme Court held that primary and secondary education financed by a local (property) tax was *prima facie* unequal and hence contrary to the federal and state constitutions. In a similar case (*Rodriguez*) U. S. Supreme Court held, rather ambiguously, that the present Texas system for financing elementary and secondary education was acceptable. Another case presenting the same issue has been recently argued before the U. S. Supreme Court, and judgment is awaited. Should the Court hold unconstitutional the type of school segregation which results from municipal boundaries that effectively produce virtually all-black schools in the city and all-white in most suburbs, then regional systems would have to emerge, presumably with regional funding. If this incidentally relieved the cities of the extra cost of compensatory education, a long step forward would have been taken toward reestablishing their economic attractiveness.

If the Federal Government Assumes All Welfare Costs—Few urban economists would dispute the assertion that, since poverty is completely mobile and able to travel wherever the welfare payments are best, *all* welfare costs, including administrative costs, should be borne by the entire country, i.e., the federal government. If the welfare tab were picked up by Washington, another long step toward reestablishing urban attractiveness would have been taken. This should include some kind of "poverty equalization factor," which would not only meet direct welfare costs, but also the extra costs of municipal housekeeping associated with rendering service to a poverty population. These extra costs include public safety, police and fire, and garbage collection (and garbage in a crowded section of the city should be collected two or three times as often as in the affluent districts).

If the State Pays the Cost of Exempt Property—Added to the cost of elementary and secondary schooling, which falls with disproportionate severity on the central cities, are the costs associated with the prevalence of tax-exempt property. The reason why so much such property is in the central area has been explained. The states should establish commissions to make educated guesses as to how much the service rendered the exempt institutions costs the municipal government. Aside from churches, the state should reimburse the city for the costs of institutions which render a social, educational, or health service to the citizens of more than one jurisdictional area. The church issue is too hot to handle, given the court rulings on the separation of church and state; and the suburbs have proportionately about as much church property as the city.

If These Costs Are Reallocated, Then What?—The breakdown of costs varies from city to city, depending on geographical size, diversity of levels of affluence, and need for special educational and welfare programs. Painting with a very broad brush, the assumption of the three elements of cost mentioned in this section by federal and/or state government would reduce many city tax bills by about half. The suburban bill would also be substantially reduced. Suburban residents would make up most of the difference through income taxation state-wide or a property tax so there would be greater equality of effort. A differential would remain between city and suburban taxes, but it would be at a lower level. Hopefully, the revised rate structure would remove one of the major disincentives to free market urban investment.

Richard E. Slitor

3

Taxation and Land Use

Introduction

Taxes have power to destroy or to buy civilization, according to the varying half-truths of our distinguished forbears. In any event, tax policy has a decided impact on patterns of land use. Some tax critics may say taxation almost literally consumes the land—meaning by that something more specific than the usual diatribe about tax burdens. How does tax policy eat up the land? This chapter attempts to count the ways.

The great decentralization movement which has been superimposed on urbanization trends in recent decades, the flight to suburbia and exurbia, central city decay, sprawl and leapfrog development, the accessible second home, and the gentleman's farm are all great land gobblers. They reflect the operation of powerful sociological, economic, and technological factors (including abundant and relatively cheap energy). The nation's tax structure cannot assume prime responsibility, but it has made important contributions to the lavish and disorderly use of land inherent in the centrifugalization of our urban centers.

The basic thrust of federal income tax inducements has been toward ownership of conventional single family homes, giving added momentum to suburban development. Part of this stimulus is toward more spacious lots and acreage than would otherwise be consumer-feasible. The poten-

RICHARD E. SLITOR *is a private economic consultant specializing in taxation and public finance. He served for over 30 years as economist for the U. S. Treasury Department in relation to housing and land use and has been Professor of Economics, Graduate Faculty, the University of Massachusetts. He has prepared special studies on taxation for the National Commission on Urban Problems, the Rand Corporation, and the Department of Housing and Urban Development. Mr. Slitor is the author of numerous books, articles, and academic papers in economics.*

tial of condominium or cooperative-type apartment ownership which extends the income tax benefits of owner tenure to high-density land use has only recently begun to emerge.

Property taxes have accentuated centrifugal trends in various ways. Tax assessment is often on the basis of less than the best and highest use of land. This slows economic adaptation to the highest and best use. Moreover, the impact of property taxes on land has not altered the supply of land, which is fixed, but the tax burden on man-made capital outlays has restrained capital commitments for buildings and improvements. This has militated against investment needed for more intensive use of land. The result is a thinning of the proportion of man-made capital to land in the land-capital mix. This thinning generally means spread and sprawl in land use.

In the income tax area, another standout is the real estate tax shelter device, rooted in highly leveraged financing plus liberal tax depreciation formulas and the possibility of repeated rounds of tax depreciation write-offs on the same property by successive "generations" of investors. This has stimulated some multi-family housing development. It has also assisted the concomitant commercial and rental housing development which accommodates the basic sprawl trend. Part of this accommodation is the apparent revitalization of the central city with high-rise offices and related commercial and residential construction. Another aspect is the creation of suburban shopping plazas and related facilities for the support of suburban living. Some variety is added to this general pattern by the occasional suburban high-rise spurred by the tax shelter device in tandem with the windfall profits attendant upon rezoning to permit conversion of low-density suburban land into more valuable sites for high-density utilization.

Property Taxation

The existing impact and potential of property taxation relating to land use have been widely recognized. Both states and localities are involved. States determine the general patterns to be applied by the local governmental jurisdictions—the primary revenue recipients—and increasingly participate in the administration of the property tax. If the states are to be the initiating and controlling agencies in land-use reform, property tax changes in the interest of improved land utilization may be one of the important instruments to be used. The treatment of the property tax under the federal income tax, specifically deductibility by homeowners, is significant in modifying its ultimate burden and land-use effects.

DOUBLE DUALITY OF THE PROPERTY TAX

The dual nature of the property tax is reflected in two separate aspects. (1) It is both a business tax and a tax on housing consumption. (2) Part of the real burden of the tax rests upon the "pure" land value component of real estate values; part of it is borne by the man-made capital investments, chiefly buildings and other land improvements, which are necessarily made in any intensive use of the land.

The property tax increases the cost of, or reduces the return to, capital investments required in land utilization. This is true even if applied at uniform rates and with consistent valuation assessment procedures to land and man-made capital instruments. Actually, land values tend to be under-assessed so that the tax bears more heavily upon the man-made capital investment component. The reduction in the return to land is without general effects on land supply. But the compression of net yields restricts the related man-made capital until its after-tax return is brought into alignment with alternative uses for mobile capital. Pre-tax rates of return on man-made capital subject to property tax are thus raised to absorb the tax while the flow of capital elsewhere reduces returns in non-property tax areas.

EXCESS BURDEN EFFECTS

In the adjustment process just described, land is utilized less intensively and less efficiently than otherwise. The apologists for high property taxes are usually silent about the "excess burden" effects, the distortions of investment away from optimal patterns, and the adverse "externalities" which add hidden costs that accompany this process and increase the burden of the tax to society:

—the obstacles to urban renewal due to the encouragement to hold on to decrepit buildings and the discouragement of new construction;
—the disincentive to maintenance and rehabilitation, with consequent impetus to the spiralling process of urban deterioration;
—the inducement to smaller structures with consequent sacrifice of the potential benefits of larger construction economies which would permit lower per cubic foot costs;
—barriers to vertical growth and more intensive land use with consequent spur to horizontal expansion and attendant social costs of sprawl in terms of transportation, sewer and water supply, and other services.[1]

Since the property tax ranges up to 2.5 or 3 percent a year (sometimes more) on fair market value in the more populous sections of the country which accounts for a large portion of its industrial and residential investment, it is evident that these excess burden effects are substantial. Housing being by nature a capital-intensive form of industry with a large part of the gross receipts consisting of return on capital, a property tax of 2.5 or

[1] The foregoing discussion owes much to an analysis in C. Lowell Harriss, "Property Taxation," Ch. 15, *Modern Fiscal Issues*, pp. 296–302. See also the same author's "Property Taxation: What's Good and What's Bad," *Challenge, The Magazine of Economic Affairs*, September–October 1973.

3 percent represents the equivalent of an excise or sale tax in the vicinity of 25 to 35 percent of the gross rental value of housing.

The property tax may also constitute a substantial element in the cost of professional, commercial, and industrial operations involving the use of buildings. It produces erratic impacts on the prices paid by consumers, depending upon the relative importance of property-taxed investment in furnishing the end-product or service. The equity results in the distribution of the burden are generally bad. The impact on economic efficiency and rational land use is probably worse.

DIFFERENTIAL ASSESSMENT OF LAND AND BUILDINGS

We have just seen how property tax reduces the intensiveness of land use by decreasing the relative amount of building and improvements in the land-capital mix. This results in more expansive, horizontal growth. It thus contributes to the process of economic decentralization and suburban sprawl which has characterized urban development and land-use patterns in the postwar decades. This analysis, by and large, has implicitly assumed that land and building values are in fact equally taxed in a given location. In reality, uniform assessment of land and building values very frequently does not occur. Land tends to be assessed at a lower figure in relation to fair market value than are the buildings or other improvements. This inequality prevails whether the practice is to assess property at a customary fraction of fair market value or at a full 100 percent of market figure. Relative underassessment of land takes various forms. One, but not the only, factor in land underassessment is the tendency not to value land in its highest and best use but to reach evaluation in terms of its current, possibly inferior, use.

The result is an accentuation of the tax impact on capital investment in buildings and other improvements. The pattern of events is familiar. The overall tax base tends to be narrowed by the omission of some of the land value components. The tax rate must therefore be higher to reach a given revenue target. In some situations investors recognize the implicitly higher effective rate of tax on improvements than on site value and respond in the classic way by reducing their building investment in relation to land. The supply of land is not affected by these adjustments but the man-made capital investment component is held back. As compared with a system of uniform assessment and taxation of land and improvements, the initial impact of higher tax rates is greater reduction of after-tax rates of return on capital. Pre-tax rates of return on these investments are driven higher than otherwise in order to cover both tax and acceptable after-tax return. Capital has to earn premium rates in heavily taxed uses and to do so it has to be kept "scarce" in these uses. This enhances the spread and sprawl effects of property tax on land use. A property tax system which bore more heavily on site values and less heavily on man-made capital would ease the deterrent pressure on buildings and improvements. The present system tends to do just the opposite.

PROPERTY TAX EXEMPTIONS

Effects—The large revenue obtained from the real property tax as the mainstay of local government finance calls for a broad, intact base. Unfortunately, the tax rests on a base that is considerably narrowed by numerous exemptions and exceptions. This of course means higher tax rates than would be necessary if the integrity of the base were better preserved. The exemptions can be of material influence—both direct and indirect—on economic behavior and land-use decisions. Paradoxically, the granting of exemptions and exceptions itself enhances (1) the economic behavioral influence of the existing exemptions or exceptions, (2) the disincentive effect of the tax itself on man-made capital investment, and (3) the natural taxpayer drive to escape tax by whatever adjustments are feasible. The reason for this effect is that at the decision-making margin each narrowing of the base entails a higher rate of tax to achieve given desired revenue goals.

Rising Trend of Exemptions—There has been a decided trend in the past century toward proliferation of exemptions and the expansion of the exemptions as a percentage of the potential real estate value base. A 1968 study developed the following data on the growth of tax exempt real property:

	1880	*1922*	*1961*	*1968*
	(Estimates of market value in $ billions)			
All Real Property	$43.6	$176.4	$1263.7	$1748.6
Exempt Real Property	$ 2.0	$ 20.5	$ 294.7	$ 569.5
Percent Exemption	4.6%	11.7%	23.4%	32.6%

Source: Harold B. Meyers, "Tax Exempt Property: Another Crushing Burden for the Cities," *Fortune* (May 1969) p. 79. Cited in "The Erosion of the Ad Valorem Real Estate Tax Base," Report of the Property Taxation Committee, National Tax Association—Tax Institute of America, 1973, p. 3.

Estimates of the ratio of exempt property to total real estate property range around one-third, the proportion varying widely among the different states.[2]

Impact on Tax Rates—Shrinkage of the effective tax base by one-third

[2] "The Erosion of the Ad Valorem Real Estate Tax Base," Report of the Property Taxation Committee, Arthur P. Becker, Chairman, National Tax Association—Tax Institute of America, *Tax Policy*, Vol. XL, No. 1, 1973, pp. 4–5.

requires a 50 percent increase in the otherwise applicable property tax rate to produce the same revenue. Thus a base of $100X at a 2 percent rate yields revenue of $2X; with the base narrowed to $66⅔X, the rate must be increased to 3 percent to produce a revenue of $2X.

There are, it is true, some offsets. Social benefits and services produced by the tax-exempt operation may save some spending by the local government, enhance surrounding land values and therefore the revenue base, and attract income and spending from the rest of the economic system. Frequently, however, these relationships are tenuous; and competitive exemptions in other jurisdictions may cancel out the local "booster" effect.

Types of Property Tax Exemptions—The range of property tax exemptions is wide: (1) governmental bodies, including federal, state, and local levels, and their authorities often engaged in semi-public, semi-private economic enterprise and development; (2) non-profit organizations, including those dedicated to education, religion, charitable activities, and welfare; (3) special groups of individuals, including veterans, widows, disabled persons, senior citizens, and other homeowners; and (4) favored businesses, industrial enterprises, and agriculture.

Some Specific Land Use Effects—Whether the rationale of exemptions is (1) conformity with the principle of intergovernmental immunity, (2) the elimination of the "pointless" circuit whereby a local government inflates tax collections and expenditures to pay its own taxes, (3) encouragement and cost sharing activities which lighten some of the burden of government, or (4) humanitarian assistance to the needy or distressed, the practical effect is almost always a tax subsidy. The subsidy of property tax exemption in reality constitutes a form of hidden expenditure on specific uses of land and related structures.

Property tax exemption helps the worthy cause only to the degree the recipient's operations involve use of real estate and on the condition that it own that real estate. Since the tax subsidy process is one so directly related to the carrying of a normal cost of using real estate, it clearly is related to a specific form of resource allocation more incontrovertibly than the much publicized federal income-tax-expenditure system under attack by fiscal reformers in recent years.

The removal of property tax obligations has the effect of encouraging the use of land and structures in endeavors which would not otherwise "pay the freight" or would not be economically feasible on the scale stimulated by the property tax exemption benefit. Ownership tenure is of course necessary to achieve this result, since mere use of rental property by a tax-exempt organization does not qualify the owner or tenant for tax benefits. The over-all economic consequence is use of scarce land resources in a manner which does not involve full cost accounting in the determination of resource use and combination proportions.

Tax Exemption and Budget Decisions on Land Use—Even from the standpoint of public budgeting and funding decisions, the social cost of operations conducted by the taxing jurisdiction itself using tax-exempt land and buildings is understated by the omission of property taxes from the calculation. Land dedicated, however meritoriously, to the public schools or hospitals is land which yields no property tax. The property tax foregone by this diversion of land from alternative taxable uses is a cost of public education as truly as the salaries, equipment, and fuel expenses of educational facilities. There is no taxpayer inequity since the effects on the distribution of costs to be borne by taxes (except for possible short-run differences in the recognition of costs and the budgetary response thereto) would be the same whether or not the county paid its own property tax on school or other property.

Property taxes reflect a social cost of using property. If they are not included in the perceived cost of certain uses, such as that for streets or schools, errors in resource allocation will result. More land and buildings tend to be allocated for tax-exempt uses than otherwise. Three interrelated but distinguishable sources of enlarged expenditure on land and buildings result from the tax-exemption arrangement:

1. Public services such as education are expanded because a major cost item, the land and buildings, is underpriced. This affects the decisions of the managers of the public funds.
2. In the mix of factors or economic resources producing a given amount of the governmental service, land and buildings will be used more liberally than other components because their use is underpriced due to the tax-exempt feature.
3. Ownership tenure as against rental occupancy becomes a "must."
4. In the budgetary process, expenditure items using real estate (land and buildings) have an illusion of cheapness.

Distortions in the Subsidy Process—It is extremely difficult and hazardous to fault a feature of the property tax law—the exemption of property of churches, universities, museums, hospitals, and numerous other welfare organizations which occupy such an honored status in our society—because it seems to accomplish what it is supposed to accomplish. But encouraging use of self-owned real estate by these organizations is not identical with encouraging them in their general functions.

Exemption is a special form of financial aid which is effective only in proportion to self-owned real estate use. It tends to distort the relative use of real property, other forms of capital, and labor. It probably encourages continued traditional patterns of operation by the exempt organizations —patterns which would not survive the test of the market place and which do not necessarily best serve the ends to which the institutions are dedicated.

URBAN DEVELOPMENT EFFECTS

The inherent effect of the property tax (even if levied at equal effective rates on land and buildings values) is not neutral, as we have seen. Land supplies are unaffected. But there is a deterrent to the construction of buildings which must earn a satisfactory return on investment after tax to compete with alternative uses outside the property tax gambit. Partly because of the way improvements are taxed, many areas are held in low use. This effect of discouraging more intensive site development promotes leapfrog development and urban sprawl.[3] This impact is enhanced to the extent that more favorable tax rates are available in new suburban areas or there are other special tax-related hindrances to construction on the closer-in sites.

COMMUNITY DECISION EFFECTS

The property tax, within the institutional context in which it functions, is open to the criticism that it has a distorting influence on community decisions which in turn influence land use. We have already examined the budget decision aspects. Another is the influence, sometimes asserted and as often denied, of income tax deductibility by homeowners in encouraging community decisions favoring over-reliance on the property tax. Another is the phenomenon sometimes called fiscal zoning.

The Lure of Income Tax Deductibility—Despite the underlying drive toward tax minimization, there is ground for believing that property taxes are sometimes pushed to otherwise unacceptable levels by the fact of income tax deductibility. Affluent suburbanites are likely to be less resistant to 2.5 and 3 percent property tax rates (on full capital value each year) since income tax deductibility may well shift 50 to 70 percent of the burden to the federal revenues (and some additional if the state has an income tax). The high property tax rates which such taxpayers are prepared to pay are considerably less tolerable for the lower-bracket resident, particularly the occasional "non-itemizer."

Collective consumption financed by an appropriately localized property tax which can be "taken off" income tax offers some interesting possibilities. One is an exclusionary effect on potential newcomers who are less well equipped to use the deduction feature. A second effect is the blunting locally of the economic tendency to deter man-made capital outlays and home improvements, examined earlier.

Fiscal Zoning—The Regional Plan Association has outlined some of the serious problems attributable to the property tax as disclosed in its re-

[3] *Financing Schools and Property Tax Relief—a State Responsibility*, Advisory Commission on Intergovernmental Relations, Ch. VI, p. 78.

search on development patterns in the New Jersey-New York-Connecticut urban region.[4]

One is the distortion of local planning. "Home rule" in planning and zoning is justified on the ground that local people should have the right to determine the kind of community they want and desire to live in. However, debates on planning and zoning ordinances seem to focus almost entirely on property tax effects in relation to the public (especially school) expenditure requirements expected to flow from alternative zoning decisions.

Tax-restraining zoning techniques involve favoring (1) one-family houses on lots of a half acre or more, to keep down the number of families with school age children and assure that each has a substantial house for tax assessment, (2) apartments with units too small to allow many school children, and (3) industry and commerce.

A range of unfortunate consequences for land use have occurred because of the combination of zoning and high property tax rates, including:

—lag in low- and moderate-income housing construction,
—sprawl and community inaccessibility due to overly liberal use of land,
—limited housing choice,
—higher cost of delivery of certain public services (fire protection, water, sewer, transportation, etc.) because of sprawl and large-lot zoning,
—and misarrangement of job locations and commercial facilities (in which commercial and industrial "ratables" spread along every highway, factories jump far into the countryside, and office buildings fail to be clustered as they should be for efficiency in compact planned centers).

URBAN BLIGHT AND ABANDONMENT

The role of the property tax in discouraging rehabilitation of rental housing, and to some extent of other types of property, is magnified as property tax rates rise as they have in decaying urban areas where costs of municipal service can rise out of proportion to the tax base.

Where expenditures are made to rehabilitate old buildings, a corresponding addition to the assessed value of the improvement should be the normal, expected result. However, a substantial rehabilitation may tend to precipitate a whole new assessment of the underlying property. Such action can result in a considerably greater increment in property tax than the added tax on the rehabilitation outlay itself. The tax increase may nearly or completely wipe out the added net return expected from the rehabilitation. Special income tax treatment may encourage rehabilitation, but the property tax effects tend to stand as a hurdle which other stimuli must help the investor to surmount.

The role of property tax collection procedures in tax delinquency situa-

4 Statement of the Regional Plan Association to the New Jersey Tax Committee, December 1970.

tions is far from innocent in the dreary procession of blighted urban structures through various stages of dilapidation into boarded-up derelicts. The possibility of "milking" rundown buildings for whatever they may pay above minimal operating outlays is enhanced by the opportunities for protracted postponement and eventual escape from property tax payments.

AGRICULTURAL LAND IN TRANSITION

Agricultural land values are often pushed up by subdivision activity and residential construction in the vicinity. In such cases tax assessment based on the value determined by the potential for immediate or future subdivision can impose a severe financial burden on the owner who seeks to continue agricultural use. At some point the heavy property tax payments will force the farmer or dairyman to fold up and sell out at a profit rather than continue losing operations or incur indebtedness to meet the cash flow requirements of paying the property tax. This may be viewed as a cause of disorderly and environmentally disruptive change which hastens horizontal growth and suburban sprawl.

On the other hand, if tax policy unbends by permitting the farm property to continue to be assessed on the basis of its value in agricultural production, the result may be to slow and divert normal expansion of residential areas. Development is then forced further out than otherwise. The special tax relief subsidizes the continued holding of property to await more intensive development, in anticipation of further appreciation.

This phase of property tax policy indeed poses a dilemma. Slowing the conversion from agricultural to more intensive use shifts the expansion process elsewhere. It stimulates further price increases on other plots. Accelerating conversion by allowing property taxes to reflect the social cost of continued holding of the land in an "inferior" use seems to put the government on the side of change which may appear to be disruptive.

Legislative action providing forebearance on agricultural land assessment is frequently justified on grounds that it serves the public interest to:

—maintain a readily available source of food and dairy products near metropolitan areas at relatively low social cost,
—preserve green open space and related environmental values at relatively low social cost,
—prevent the forced conversion of such open space to more intensive uses as a result of tax pressures incompatible with the practical use of such land for farms,
—and reserve relatively unspoiled areas for future more leisurely development consistent with longer range goals of land use, thus avoiding commitments to intensive use which could not subsequently be reversed without substantial capital sacrifice and community resistance.

Apart from questions of inter-personal equity, the agricultural land preference is suspect on several specific grounds relating to optimal land-use policy:

1. It offers too easy a haven for the land speculator who can achieve lower carrying costs for his speculative holdings by meeting in one way or another the statutory requirements for a bona fide agricultural operation.[5]
2. Extensive additional holding of otherwise available subdivision land off the market enhances the rise in prices of other land at public expense. The general body of taxpayers are required to pay higher tax rates both to provide the services for a growing community and to make up for the tax subsidy to the agricultural "holdouts."
3. The land impacted most heavily by potential property tax increases will usually be close in. This is the land that can be held in agricultural use because of the exemption. Therefore, the property tax relief pushes development out further horizontally than if it occurred where market forces would determine. Since the pattern of continued holding for agricultural use is likely to be irregular, leapfrog development is likely to result. The cost of public services for the new, further-out communities will be greater than if development were more regular.

Federal Income Tax Structure

The impact of the federal income tax on land use is wide. It affects many actors in the drama of housing supply and use, commercial construction, agriculture, and land speculation. It operates through various tax mechanisms and linkages. It is for the most part inadvertent—tax effects have flowed in large measure from provisions of the law which were not consciously designed to modify or distort land use in the ways they have. Nevertheless, sprawl, artificial land scarcity, leapfrog development, high property turnover rates, and urban blight have all been their unintended by-products. Homeowners, multi-family housing syndicators, land speculators, residential and commercial investors and their entourage, farmers and gentleman tax shelter farmers, slumlords and urban revitalizers—all have felt the magnetic pull and titillation of the tax dollar saved via adroit use of land and its improvements.

While the property tax inhibits intensive land use involving investment exposure to the tax, the federal income tax (and largely parallel features of the typical state income tax) has both dampening and reinforcing impacts:

[5] States providing this relief may specify certain criteria of bona fide agricultural use such as the applicable zoning, present and past use of the land, and its productivity including uses as timberland and reforestation areas. See, for example, Maryland Annotated Code Sec. 19, Art. 81, as reported in Consumers Clearing House, State Tax Reporter, Maryland, Vol. 1, para. 20–164, pp. 2119–2120.

—the deductibility of property tax for income tax purposes reduces its effective burden both on land and on the owner-occupied home,

—depreciation, capital gain, homeowner benefits, and other features stimulate investment and land use in ways which, broadly speaking, spell out a pattern of horizontal growth and sprawl, with accompanying waste and disorder.

Property tax varies of course from locality or region to another, so that it has geographic differentials and locational impacts. One jurisdiction can compete with another in terms of property tax requirements relative to community services furnished. Federal income tax effects, by contrast, are essentially uniform nationwide, subject only to the pattern of geographical distribution of activities or property income sources which may enjoy federal tax preferences.

DEPRECIATION ON BUILDINGS AND THE REAL ESTATE TAX SHELTER

A key tax impact on land use is exercised by the accelerated depreciation methods[6] allowed on buildings, including rental housing, hotels and motels, offices, shopping plazas and malls, and industrial construction. These allowances in combination with highly leveraged mortgage financing gave rise to the well-known real estate shelter device.

Depreciation—in contrast with other expenses of operating real estate, such as mortgage interest, repairs and maintenance, utility services, property taxes, and operating personnel—is not an out-of-pocket expense representing an actual cash outflow from the operation. It is merely an accounting set-aside, representing the fact that the building will eventually be used up or become obsolete and at some estimated future date will need to be demolished and replaced.

Depreciation allowances based on the entire cost of the property are large in relation to a relatively thin margin of equity investment in mortgaged-financed real estate. They normally exceed any realistic estimate of the actual decline in usefulness (or value) of the property in the early years. They typically eliminate any taxable net income on the leveraged investment. The net loss they frequently generate from a well-designed tax shelter spills over and may be used to offset or "shelter" other sources of income.

As the depreciation allowances decline, the tax shelter becomes less effective; and the property may be resold at a capital gain, reflecting both possible appreciation of the land and building and the excess depreciation

[6] For the post-1969 period, these are 200 percent declining balance or sum of the years-digits for the new residential buildings; 150 percent declining balance for other new buildings; and 125 percent declining balance for subsequent-owner rental housing with a remaining useful life of 20 years or more. All subsequent-owner nonresidential buildings and residential buildings with a useful life under 20 years are limited to the straightline method.

taken without corresponding decline in value. The next buyer repeats the process using a shorter remaining life to offset the loss of the accelerated methods.

The real estate cycle thus represents "borrowing" of the income tax savings on the depreciation at ordinary rates without interest and repaying only part of the loan representing the depreciation calculated as capital gain, years later, and again without interest. Conversion of ordinary into long-deferred capital gains is thus the essence of the operation. "Recapture," or the partial recapture, i.e., the taxing of some of the gain reflecting prior overdepreciation at ordinary rather than capital gains tax rates, has moderated but far from eliminated, the tax advantage. Even full recapture would still permit the lengthy deferment of tax. At present discount rates the deferral represents a greater advantage than in the fifties and early sixties.

This device stimulates construction. It also encourages instability of tenure by causing the turnover of properties so that the next owner, having reestablished the depreciable basis at the sale price, can repeat the process, although possibly at a lower level.

The depreciation allowances on buildings have been cut back under the Tax Reform Act of 1969, but they remain liberal, particularly for housing. Recapture rules on gain from sale of depreciable real property have also been tightened under the 1969 tax reform legislation. Nevertheless, the real estate tax shelter device has not entirely lost its charm. Tightening the rules of the game has made it necessary for the aggressive seeker of tax shelters to look more closely at the finer points and readapt to the new, tighter framework.

Depreciable Cost Allocation—The income tax law, perhaps more than before the 1969 reform, places a premium on placing a high valuation on the building or improvements (which are depreciable) and a low valuation on land (which is not depreciable for income tax purposes). This tends to put pressure on the property tax assessor to allocate more of the appraised value to the depreciable investment and less to land. By doing so, he can assist the local investor in economizing on federal income tax payments to a distant Internal Revenue collector. Regrettably this side-effect worsens the impact on the property tax in relieving site value and burdening active investment in improvements.

Land-use Effects—The over-all impact of this untidy complex of tax laws is, interestingly enough, one of "simultaneously encouraging slum deterioration in the cities and encouraging urban sprawl in the suburbs." [7] Depreciation tax savings create a built-in incentive for quick turnover,

[7] Robert A. Levine, "San Jose, the Urban Crisis, and the Feds," paper prepared for presentation before the Legislative Action Committee, U. S. Conference of Mayors, San Jose, California, May 15, 1972, p. 6.

getting in and out with minimum maintenance. Initial construction may be designed with this in mind, without regard to the longer-run economies of better construction. The old-fashioned virtues of long-range property stewardship tend to be sacrificed. Tenement owners buy up buildings, obtain the quick tax advantages of rapid depreciation, and then sell to another owner who repeats the cycle with minor variations.

The possibility of allocating land value to depreciable basis tends to artificially perpetuate the continued use of old rundown buildings as tax-saving vehicles, some of which have an overall property value that would otherwise be less than the worth of the bare land. In effect, land value is depreciated and redepreciated by successive owners. The practice makes it economic for investors to keep in use buildings otherwise overdue for demolition merely because they can qualify for periodic apportionment of a fictitious depreciation base for income tax purposes.

Depreciation allowances thus have apparently conflicting effects on construction and the urban landscape. They increase the supply of new buildings but prolong the life of the old.

The depreciation provisions—which might in isolation be expected to stimulate vertical growth counter to the general horizontality of tax incentive effects—is ideally designed to promote suburban commercial developments, shopping malls, office buildings, as well as high rise apartments. The tax laws thus support the suburban commercial investment needed to serve the sprawling population distribution encouraged by the homeowner tax benefits. This general effect predominates over the tax-sheltered oases of urban revitalization in the form of the towering modern office structures and commercial development appearing in the center of the older downtown areas.

TAX ADVANTAGES FOR HOMEOWNERS

The federal income tax (and the typical state income tax structure) assures important income tax benefits for owner-occupied housing. These are generally regarded as increasing housing consumption relative to other unsubsidized components of the consumer budget. Homeowner tax advantages comprise three interrelated elements:

—the exclusion from the concept of taxable income of the net imputed rental value (gross rental value less repairs, maintenance, insurance, and depreciation),
—the deduction from this narrowed income concept of mortgage interest payments, and
—the deduction of property tax payments.

Smaller consumer benefits accrue to renters in the form of additional rental housing supplies and therefore lower rents, reflecting the accelerated tax depreciation allowances given to rental housing investors, and the competition of owner-occupancy as an alternative supply mechanism. Over-all, however, the direct tax benefits for homeowners outweigh the indirect, pass-through benefits to tenants. There remains, then, the equity issue of balance in the tax treatment of homeowner and tenant, a favorite theme of postwar tax reform literature.

The anti-homeowner bias of conventional tax reform doctrine—about as much anti-middle class as it is pro-tax uniformity—dwells upon the income tax benefits for homeowners as tax subsidies which: (1) favor tax-payers whose economic circumstances and mode of earning a living make it possible to own a home; (2) adversely affect resource allocation by over-stimulating housing consumption, including second homes, luxury features, such as swimming pools, tennis courts, barbecue patios, etc., which involve expansive use of land; and (3) contribute to the growth of the sprawling suburbs and doughnut-shaped cities which characterize the present economically wasteful form of human settlement and land utilization for metropolitan living.[8]

Little is said by the tax reform school about the favorable social externalities of owner occupancy. The rationale for encouraging home-ownership under the income tax law is in fact a substantial one, despite the efforts of the tax reformers to brush it aside.

The tax policy objectives of the present federal income tax rules in this area go beyond upgrading housing and fostering civic virtue or a sense of stability and identity with the community. Family economic security in a troubled, insecure, and economically unstable world is promoted in a major way if the family owns its own home. Tenancy tends to be the most socially costly form of housing since it affords little if any incentive to careful usage and day-to-day maintenance by the occupant. The tenant, especially if fortified with a modicum of alienated psychology, tends to give the property hard, indifferent usage, too often bordering upon vandalism. The social costs of housing would rise enormously if the whole housing complex were shifted to universal tenant tenure.

Ownership tenure eliminates the risk-inflated rates of return and management compensation to equity owners required for rental housing. The owner can in effect earn this return on his own commitment rather than having to pay it to a landlord investor. It also obviates the social cost of administering and adjudicating landlord-tenant relations in a judicial system which functions at conspicuously less than ideal efficiency and at considerable cost.

Homeownership affords opportunities for do-it-yourself projects. These permit use of the spare time of the owner and his family in creating wealth and income. From the standpoint of the homeowner, these may yield only

8 Point 3 is stressed, for example but without regard to the causative role of taxation, by Daniel Rose in an article entitled "The Economic Future of New York City," New York *Times,* November 25, 1973, p. F-12.

a modest net gain over and above the personal or psychic cost of his efforts; but from the social standpoint, it is essentially the gross contribution of wealth and saving of resources needed for home repair and improvement which counts as the beneficial externality.

Homeownership adds inflation hedging with respect to a basic part of the household budget. Not entirely external to the housing decision and the related market forces, it is clearly a significant part of the rationale of social policy regarding the taxation of homeowners. Having failed signally in the art of achieving reasonable price stability, society should at least strive to help people to live with the chronic inflation process, narrow the area which may need rent or similar administrative controls, and possibly reduce pressures for continuing cost and price escalation.

Even if homeowner tax benefits boost land and housing consumption, the latter reduces housing costs in this largely unexplored range of ways. For those concerned with land use, the present situation leaves an uneasy balance between the substantial social and economic advantages of widespread homeownership on the one hand and the equity problems and overexpansive land consumption attributable to the present tax set-up.

CAPITAL GAINS TAX AND LAND USE

The traditional concessions to long-term capital gains under the federal income tax, designed primarily with the fluidity of organized security markets in mind, have a substantial impact on land use.

Despite the tightening of tax preferences in recent years, capital gains of individuals are taxed at no more than half the applicable income tax rate and frequently less than half on the sizeable portion of gains of affluent investors still qualifying for a 25 percent ceiling rate. Corporations also enjoy a maximum rate well below the ordinary top rate.

Unrealized capital gains held until the individual bequeaths the underlying property to his heirs are entirely exempted from even capital gains tax. The tax basis is automatically stepped up to fair market value at the time of estate tax valuation, thus canceling out the unrealized appreciation for income tax purposes. The estate or the heirs may sell the property without income tax on the gain which was accumulated during the period the property was held by the previous owner.

Stimulus to Land Speculation—One major effect is the substantial incentive this tax structure gives to land speculation as compared with other economic activities which generate ordinary income taxed at regular rates. This adds an additional income tax fillip to the boost given speculative land holdings by the underassessment of "underutilized" land for property tax purposes. The ultimate reward is taxed cheaply under the income tax; the costs of attaining it are lowered by favorable property tax treatment. Carrying costs are further absorbed up to as much as 70 percent (more in some states) by the income tax deductibility of property tax and mortgage interest on speculative land holdings.

Exemption of Unrealized Gains in the Estate—The land-use impact of this area of the tax system is further complicated by the internally inconsistent and inadvertent effects of the capital gains tax rules. The lower rate is designed to encourage market fluidity and willingness of owners to realize speculative gains once they have materialized and their rate of accrual no longer justifies further holding. But the potential exemption of unrealized gains means that it becomes advantageous purely for tax reasons to hang on to property beyond the otherwise advantageous time of sale. The capital gains tax preference is thus brought into a competitive juxtaposition with a zero alternative rate rather than the higher ordinary tax rate. Wealthy elderly landowners become "frozen into" their holdings, seeking to pass their gains intact and income tax-free to their heirs.

Astute middle-aged investors may deliberately seek out land investment as a vehicle to build up non-taxable accruals to their net worth which may some day be passed on to their heirs without even capital gains tax. The tax differential between this kind of wealth accumulation and the hard route of saving out of ordinary income after tax, or even of successful investment in securities which need to be sold before the unrealized appreciation may be swallowed up by the vicissitudes of the stock market, is remarkable, even in a tax structure marked by deliberate preferences and anomalies.

The freezing of land holdings for income tax-exempt transfer to heirs may block normal patterns of land use and community development for decades, creating artificial scarcities, higher land prices, and irregular patterns of sprawl and leapfrog growth.

SCENIC AND ENVIRONMENTAL EASEMENTS

One of the instruments of public policy for preserving scenic beauty and carrying out environmental purposes is the set of income tax provisions relating to the donation (and bargain sale equivalent to partial gift) of scenic and other environmental easements to conservation trusts and public bodies. Such easements are equivalent to covenants whereby the owner of real estate accepts restrictions on its use such as limitations on the height of buildings constructed on it, its preservation as open space, or granting public access to it under specified conditions.

Charitable contributions in kind are generally valued at their fair market value, and the ability to deduct donations of environmental easements on that basis provides important tax savings to the donor. Such savings would partially compensate him for the sacrifice of unfettered use of the property and thus provide an incentive for land use in accordance with environmental objectives.

Treasury procedures in implementing the valuation of environmental easements in various types of situations and certain restrictions on the deductibility of such gifts introduced, possibly by inadvertence, under the Tax Reform Act of 1969 have apparently impaired the incentive value of this tax instrument.

The Tax Policy Advisory Committee to the Council on Environmental Quality addressed itself to this problem among others in 1971–72. Its Report to the Council indicated that until 1971 "the method of valuation of so-called scenic easements, by which owners of land gave to a charitable organization or to a government body a permanent right to prevent the construction of buildings, or to maintain a shoreline or otherwise limit development, was so constricted that there was little tax benefit from such contributions." [9]

The Committee then went on to state that a more liberal interpretation of the tax law was under consideration by the Treasury to permit the development of more effective programs to secure scenic easements and that the Committee had encouraged action along these lines to improve environmental quality.

Both concepts of valuation and uncertainties about the value ultimately accepted by the tax authorities as a measure of the gift seem to be involved. Sometimes scenic easements may seem to protect the existing use— probably the highest and best for an indefinite period, for example, where it represents a beautiful and exclusive residential area—so that property value is protected and even enhanced rather than sacrificed by the grant of the easement. Also, taxpayers often hesitate to place restrictions on the use of their property for an indefinite period if they are not assured at the time of the gift what value and therefore what deduction is attached to it—an assurance which is difficult indeed to obtain where advance valuation with definitive review and approval by tax authorities is not feasible. Temporary scenic easements, which although less satisfactory than those in perpetuity may gain time for environmental and community planning agencies to secure a more lasting protection of land resources, seem to have questionable standing as a basis for a tax deduction claim under present law.

These and other difficulties have left environmentalists who are concerned with land use and with the protection of the nation's legacy of scenic beauty and earth resources both uneasy and dissatisfied.

Here the possibilities of bending the tax law to create attractive tax savings to land donors or dedicators which will serve scenic, environmental, or other meritorious public purposes have run afoul of the drive to prevent income tax manipulation and the hidden tax expenditures which reformers seek to bring into public view and to eradicate from the tax

[9] Report of the Tax Policy Advisory Committee to the Council on Environmental Quality, February 1973, p. 36.

system. Those who place environmental objectives, including scenic preservation and land conservation in various forms, above the purities of tax uniformity want exception from the tighter tax provisions for specified forms of real estate easements. They may succeed in some degree, but it seems doubtful that any such changes will revive the more objectionable forms of tax manipulation under the guise of environmental protection. Direct measures outside the tax incentive field may have to be called upon to do the job.

TAX BENEFITS FOR AGRICULTURE

A substantial array of tax provisions are of special benefit to farmers: special deductions representing the "expensing" of capital outlays, capital gain treatment on certain items of income, lenient accounting rules which permit the deduction of costs of building up inventories, and rules permitting the play-off of expense deductions of raising livestock with capital gains rates on the proceeds of their sale. Despite recent safeguards and loophole plugging aimed at tax avoidance by non-bona fide farmers, these provisions still attract affluent investors, businessmen, and professional practitioners seeking tax shelter. So-called hobby farming has long been a source of both erosion of the income tax base and in some areas serious competition for bona fide farmers and ranchers. In the citrus fruit industry the deduction of development costs apparently resulted at times in speculative planting, overproduction, and waste.

As so often happens in the tax field, there is a bright side to the farm tax haven rules. They have probably been a strong stimulus to the creation and financial support of picture farms, rural showplaces, affluent beef cattle breeding operations, horse farms, and racing stables. They have also contributed to the development of citrus and almond groves and similar aspects of the nation's agricultural capacity. They are doubtless responsible for the rehabilitation of many rundown working farms, the appearance of attractive whitewashed fences, and other eye-appealing changes which improve much of our rural landscape, particularly in the general vicinity of large metropolitan centers populated by eligible tax-conscious farm investors. On the less attractive side, they have nurtured the development of a tax avoidance industry which literally peddled participation by high-bracket absentee owners in the raising of fine beef and breeding cattle. Some of these beef cattle operations were inherently uneconomic and virtually dependent upon the tax subsidy. Some have collapsed of their own weight or folded with the slightest doubt as to their acceptability.

These are the highlights of the enormously complex and essentially unsatisfactory state of the law applicable to hobby-suspect and tax-shelter agricultural operations. Despite occasional declarations that the farm tax shelter is in ruins, substantial tax avoidance opportunities remain. Some farm groups still call for tax reform legislation to restrict tax-loss farming and investment in farming by non-farm individuals and corporations to gain tax advantages. The structure still tends to support an artificial sector of the industry in the hot-house environment of the tax haven.

A superficially brighter, more decorative, and prosperous-looking farm countryside is purchased at the cost of taxpayers generally. Along with inflation, the structure helps bid up land prices to reflect the capitalized value of expected tax benefits. It also supports the retention of land in speculative holding patterns and uses which would not be economically desirable or feasible for ordinary farmers. The overall result is a less flexible and less efficient use of agricultural land, along with resource malallocation, since hobby farmers and tax shelter seekers are not paragons of economy. The fact that not all farm operations lend themselves to the major tax avoidance opportunities complicates the resource distortions.

Estate and Gift Taxes

The estate and gift taxes are by their nature taxes on wealth. More specifically, their economic incidence is on savings. Financing government by estate and gift tax revenue is tantamount to channeling savings into the payment of government operating expenses. If liquid savings of the decedent are not available to pay the estate tax, assets are liquidated by the estate to absorb capital funds from the capital market in competition with new security issues for capital development purposes.

Assets which individuals have accumulated or developed through their lifetimes may need to be liquidated to meet estate tax liabilities. If non-liquid assets are readily divisible and marketable, there is relatively little economic dislocation in paying estate tax. If the estate is illiquid and contains substantial assets which cannot be partially liquidated to meet tax liabilities, there may be hardship.

Some types of assets may be passed on to the next generation by means of gifts, which are taxable at a lower rate than bequests, are eligible for a $3,000 annual exclusions per recipient, and are covered by a $30,000 cumulative lifetime exemption on gifts above the $3,000 per donee annual exclusion. Farms and sizeable indivisible landholdings are not always readily adaptable to the gradual gift method of intergenerational transfer.

The complex impact of the estate and gift tax structure on land use is not open to facile generalization. It does involve appreciable effects on family holdings which may include substantial real estate components:

—The necessity for eventually meeting estate taxes puts pressure on the prudent owner to accumulate and maintain a greater degree of liquidity, a pressure which may tend to starve the farm or business operation for capital funds needed for improvement and expansion.

—Payment of estate tax may strip the next generation of the liquid capital reserve needed to provide working capital and a safety margin for contingencies.

—Estate tax payment problems may lead to the break-up or disposition of family farms and land holdings.

The moderate rates of estate tax on medium-sized estates, the $60,000 exemption, the marital deduction, and deferred payment relief may seem to ease these problems. But they are nevertheless real. The "gift tax route" is not as well adapted to farm and land transfers as it is to the passing of stock and other business interests. The rapid rise in land values in the expanding, inflationary economy of the postwar decades has often made it difficult to accumulate the liquidity to assure orderly transfer of farms and landholdings.

Whether good or bad from other viewpoints, estate taxation has thus had some tendency to compel break-up of farm and other unitary landholdings. There are related effects: increase in the available land in the current supply-demand equation, alteration in past patterns of land use, and accelerated subdivision and conversion of farm open space into more intensive residential use.

The estate tax savings from charitable bequests encourage transfers of real estate to eleemosynary and public use. This aspect of the estate tax mechanism is one which is responsible for many transfers which further the preservation, beautification, and conservation of our natural and cultural heritage.

William B. Shore

4

What Do the People Want?

Does Land Use Reflect What People Want?

When the hearing room is packed with people shouting "no more highways . . . give us public transportation instead," does that mean they would be willing to live at densities high enough to support public transportation and work in downtowns instead of at scattered sites?

When the highway is built and it quickly fills with traffic, does that mean people really did want it?

When most people tell a poll-taker they prefer living in a small town, but people are leaving small towns in droves, which really reflects public preference?

When majorities in all the municipalities that control the vacant land of an urban region support a zoning ban on apartments and town houses and most people in opinion polls say they want one-family houses, why is it clear to both builders and municipal authorities that apartments and town houses (in many urban regions) will fill as soon as they are built?

WHY WE DON'T KNOW WHAT PEOPLE WANT

Fitting land use to public preferences is not a simple matter.

Market forces are too piecemeal. They react only to existing conditions. People might prefer a downtown apartment *if* their job and other special activities were downtown, but they choose a suburban house when the better jobs and services are in the suburbs. Department stores and office enterprises might be better off downtown than in shopping centers and

---

Vice President of the Regional Plan Association, WILLIAM B. SHORE *has written (as co-author) the well-known book* How to Save Urban America *and television documentaries. He has also edited the* Public Administration Review.

on isolated campuses if city services were better and other businesses and apartments were going downtown.

Public opinion surveys are inadequate in the same way—"if . . . then" contingencies seldom are considered. Moreover, those polled seldom know what the trade-offs are—e.g., that good bus service cannot be provided unless households are housed at least five to the acre and jobs and services are centralized. There are dozens of dimensions to realistic alternatives.

The usual democratic process has not achieved a satisfying land-use pattern either, because decisions affecting land use are usually made without public understanding of the longer-term effects. If the day-to-day decisions are based on a long-term plan, the public seldom understands the plan or has had much impact on it.

Furthermore, in states where school finance is heavily based on local real estate taxes, the anticipated effect of development on the school tax determines land use more frequently than a vision of the good community.

Finally, many people affected by the most important land-use decisions have no political leverage on them. In some cases they do not live in the jurisdiction where the decision is made (e.g., most urban residents needing housing do not live in the locality whose land-use decisions are greatly restricting the supply). In other cases, the governmental agency making the decision has no interest in the land-use implications (e.g., few state higher-education authorities locate campuses, few highway authorities choose routes with an eye to their land-use impact).

What Is Wrong: A Summary—So land-use controls in the United States today probably fail to reflect what people would choose if they had the facts and the vote. While people control their own municipal territory, they fail to use that power to build a satisfactory land-use mosaic for the broader urban area within which they actually live and work. Above the municipal level, there is little public participation or formal legislative involvement in setting plans, and the plans that are made almost never have a direct effect on what happens. State and federal decisions that affect land use seldom are made with their land-use implications in mind. And market forces respond only to present conditions.

Right now the only consistently effective kind of public participation in land use is the small group that succeeds in stopping a project because they fear it will hurt them personally. A recent example is a proposal by the New York State Urban Development Corporation to build nine 100-unit housing projects in northern Westchester County. Not only were the projects stopped but the Corporation was emasculated. An Anthony Quayle opinion survey revealed that a majority of Westchester residents even in the towns in which the projects were to be built favored their construction. But the majority favored it as a benefit to the whole community, while the minority opposed it for personal reasons. The state legislature concluded, apparently, that the opposition felt more strongly than the supporters and would be more likely to vote on the basis of this one issue at the next election.

TO GET WHAT PEOPLE WANT

Two steps are necessary to develop America as people want it after the public assumes enough power to control the use of land more completely: (1) allocating land-use controls to the government that controls the whole area affected, and (2) making the planning process far more influential and open to informed public participation.

Now, what governmental jurisdictions should be responsible for what land-use issues and how can the planning process be improved as a basis for those decisions?

Basic Issues and Who Should Decide Them

NATIONAL PERSPECTIVE

If the ecologists are right—that the first land-use question is where not to build—then we should start land-use planning by defining those lands that should not be developed (e.g., flood plains, wetlands, steep slopes, the richest farmland) and require special permission and open hearings to make exceptions. If so, this principle should be established nationally (though it might be applied at state, county, and local levels).

We should also decide nationally whether there are any regions of the country whose resources are or might soon become overloaded. Is there an objective reason why one or another region should limit its population? Contrarily, some regions want to grow. Should national policy encourage that?

National issues of urban growth obviously must be decided by Congress: the Oregons that want to close their borders, the West Virginias that want more jobs. If Oregon can demonstrate justification for barring further growth and West Virginia can show that enlargement would bring benefits beyond the cost of diverting jobs to a place the jobs would not otherwise have gone, national policy can be set to try to achieve these goals. Now, the Oregon stance—which some deem noble just because it is anti-Babbitry—is no more justified than the rich suburb's use of police powers (i.e., zoning) to keep out middle-income people.

Perhaps there is a good national purpose to be served by closing one state or another to further development, e.g., saving wilderness. But it must be a national purpose, nationally determined, to be legitimate in a nation that was founded to preserve open borders and free trade among its several states.

Now our national growth policy consists of southern states and Puerto

Rico exporting their structural unemployment by refusing to pay adequate welfare and undeveloped states refusing to shoulder their share of national growth pressures by barring development. Both sneer at the large old cities for failing to solve "their" problems.

From the national viewpoint, this growth policy may be most "efficient," i.e., it might maximize the Gross National Product; but the policy should be made consciously and on the basis of more understanding of its effects.

REGIONAL PERSPECTIVE

Most urban regions are single housing market areas in that housing supply in one part affects supply and demand in another. Most are a single economy in that a corporation decides to come into the region first and then decides where in the region to locate. The rough pattern of major facilities, housing density, and basic transportation arteries should be set regionally because all the residents are affected. Similarly, the best location for subsidized housing should be determined regionally or all will be confined to the jurisdictions where the poor already live whether appropriate or not. In most of the United States there is no government covering a whole urban region, though almost all regions have a planning process.

METROPOLITAN PERSPECTIVE

Within large urban regions like New York, Philadelphia, Los Angeles, and Chicago, there are many potential metropolitan communities. In making land-use decisions, they could achieve a large measure of independence from adjoining metropolitan areas in the same region—if they were planned to do so—though their economy would still get its sustenance from the region's economy and the central city could remain a center for all the region's metropolitan communities. Within the framework of a regional plan, each of the metropolitan communities could set its own development pattern—where the offices and department stores, hospitals, and other large facilities go and how housing and transportation relate to them.

Within the New York Region, Regional Plan Association has recommended some two dozen metropolitan communities centered on such cities as Paterson, Bridgeport, Stamford, and White Plains. These potential metropolitan communities coincide roughly with existing county boundaries so land-use decisions could be made by existing counties. (In Connecticut, appropriate "regional" planning areas have been defined, but there is no general government between the state and municipalities to promulgate these "regional" plans.)

If recent development patterns continue, however, these will not be real communities suited to planning for themselves. Development is now scattered and unconfined to a distinct community in a pattern Regional Plan

Association has called "spread city." If spread city growth continues, urban regions will become undifferentiated pieces of real estate and not metropolitan communities. That is the basic issue facing urban regions, and it will determine the area suitable for planning.

Spread City vs. Metropolitan Centers and Communities

Spread city is homogenized urbanization made up of a seemingly random scatter—a subdivision of homes here, an apartment there; a shopping center, offices or factories at expressway interchanges or in industrial parks; and small shops, offices and services lining the main highways.

Tom Wicker of the New York *Times* described the manifestation in North Carolina this way:

> . . . Here in Charlotte as elsewhere, mass transit facilities are minimal; in addition, this city has been built outward from its own center in long glittering strings of plastic, neon, glass and ersatz. Now, for miles before a motorist reaches what used to be the city, the shopping centers, the fast-food joints, the service stations, the apartment and housing developments, the glass office buildings and the ugly mobile home sales lots line the roads in endless tribute to an illusory prosperity.[1]

There is an alternative. We could return to the urban pattern of pre-World War II—not as high density but the same pattern: putting the activities people do together in the center and ranging housing around them. Day-to-day activities such as grocery and drug stores, the local realtor and insurance agent, would locate in local centers—suburban villages or city neighborhoods. Large facilities—office enterprises, department and specialty stores, hospitals, central libraries, hotels, the arts—would locate in "metropolitan centers," serving, say, a quarter-million to two million persons. In most old urban areas, there are downtowns that could be modernized and enlarged into metropolitan centers. But recently, we have turned our backs on these instead of building on them.

By combining the many activities people do together, a magnet is created. Because people go there for many purposes, they want to be as near as possible. A social magnet attracts housing as a steel magnet attracts iron filings. If zoning allowed, housing would naturally form around the center—highest-density in the center, somewhat lower-density around the centers, tapering off to low-density at the urban edges. Everyone would have a choice: living in little space *in* the center and being near places he goes to frequently and near public transportation in every direction; or living *near* the center in a moderate amount of space, an easy bus ride or very short auto trip to the facilities he frequents; or having much more space farther away, but necessarily depending on the automobile and having much longer trips for most purposes.

1 New York *Times*, December 4, 1973.

This "magnetic field" pattern is the way to save energy. People voluntarily choose to use less land—for housing, offices and shopping—because there is an incentive to give up space. Higher density is associated with much less energy consumption—a little less for heat and a great deal less for transportation. Trips are shorter, on the average, and many more are on public transportation. By contrast, public transportation cannot work in spread city because not enough people live within walking distance of a bus stop, few people travel in the same direction to work or shop, and those who do would have to wait while the bus makes stop after stop after stop at individual buildings. Only a downtown in the center of population can support public transportation that is good enough to woo a person from his car.

The centers-and-communities pattern also saves travel throughout the day because related activities are close together.

People are led to do more: the college in the midst of other activities is more likely to attract people to continue their education, and to accommodate students who must work their way through. The museum next to the department store will be more used than one that is far away.

Natural open space is saved from random penetration. There is more distinctiveness in the appearance compared to spread city, which looks alike anywhere in the country. And the face of spread city is ugly—mainly great fields of asphalt parking, with the shops and services that line every highway shouting their wares at the speeding motorists.

The centers-and-communities pattern is more socially responsible. Many of the poor do not have cars. (In 1970 more households in the New York Region had no cars than in 1960—over half the New York City and Newark households.) Yet the best unskilled jobs, shopping, and many public services including community colleges are out of reach except by automobile. Furthermore, an urban center is a place where the two halves of society would continue to meet. It could hold us together until we are prepared for more integrated living.

Finally, this is the way to build a sense of community. In spread city, neighbors share little in common.

But there are many advantages to spread city, also. It does combine at least some urban advantages with a noncity spacious feel (one drives on highways rather than streets); the auto can go everywhere and everything is designed for the auto; in a word, spread city is convenient—usually it is new and inexpensively renewable. But the big advantage is this: there is little need for coordination. Everyone can make his own decisions, go his own way without adjusting much to others. A developer can put up a shopping center or office much more quickly than he can in a downtown renewal area; no one has to travel together—if the energy shortage does not become too bad. Spread city works well for people who do not like strangers.

LOCAL ISSUES

Within each metropolitan community, there could be many local communities of varying sizes. Location of grocery, hardware and drug stores, local realtors' and lawyers' offices, streets and the design of the whole community could be left to local governments, as long as they make these choices within the framework of the county's plan and the county makes its decisions according to the rough guidelines of the regional plan. Of course many municipal boundaries do not now conform to real local communities. Without boundary adjustments, all the people most affected would not have a voice in their local land-use decisions.

MAKING DECISIONS IN SPREAD CITY

If the pattern of centers-and-communities is chosen, there would be real communities within which land-use decisions could be made by those most affected and by no one else. If spread city is the desired pattern, only regional government could cover everyone directly affected by land-use decisions. There is no beginning and no end to the development. It goes on like a chain link fence; people travel in all directions to work, to shop, to play, to get their services. No real economic or social boundary separates one area from another. The choice for land-use decision-making is between some arbitrary local government area, accepting the fact that one locality will be making policy that affects its neighbors on all sides, or the whole region—and if the whole region, the government will have to keep growing outward as the region spreads.

Infusing Public Preferences into Plans

If an appropriate level of government makes land-use decisions in the usual democratic fashion, we can assume these decisions will reflect the public view at least as well as the political system does on other issues. However, the American political system is geared to decisions reflecting short-term interests. The elected official has an eye on the next election, a very few years away. If longer-term, comprehensive interests are to be reflected in public land-use policies, a plan is needed and a constituency must be organized that cares about the plan.

Now, how to reflect public views in the plan? To some degree it can be done without formally involving the public, and planners generally have tried to get along that way in the planning process.

WITHOUT DIRECT PUBLIC PARTICIPATION

Clear-cut Objective Legislative Criteria—If Congress or a state or county legislature could establish one simple objective criterion by which all plans could be judged, then perhaps professional planners could be entrusted with designing development to meet that standard. For example, our present situation suggests that one dominant criterion might be energy saving. Congress might determine that all regional, county, and local plans should aim at using the least possible energy. Would all planning decisions then be technical judgments that could be left to the expert planners?

The Soviet Union did something like that several years ago. National growth policy was founded on one main principle: minimizing immediate capital investment in the urban infrastructure. Planners determined that this criterion could best be met by channeling people into middle-sized urban regions, i.e., encouraging the growth of small regions and halting the growth of large regions. It worked only moderately well. Other criteria were so important to so many people that the largest regions kept growing—despite far stronger controls on residence and employment location than we would ever tolerate.

Furthermore, energy-conservation alone would be an inadequate criterion. With appropriate transportation and employment location controls, for example, large cities and small cities might be made equal in energy requirements. Then, which should we choose and where?

Some planners tell us that there is an objective measure of the best use for every piece of land—the ecological approach. But this does not answer every question objectively either. There is far more land suitable for urban uses than we are likely to need, and there are many alternative ways to use land "respectfully." Nor does the approach indicate how to trade off social and economic values against the ecological ones.

Determining What People Want by What They Do—Some planners feel that the best measure of what people want is what they do, and they try to find mathematical measures of people's behavior which can be projected into somewhat different situations as the basis for plans. In cost-benefit studies of prospective highways, for example, the benefit side is made up primarily of the dollar value of travel time that will be saved by the new highway. And what is the dollar value of travel time saved? That is derived from people's behavior—how much they seem willing to pay to travel faster—particularly by travelling on a toll road when a free road is available. What this method cannot include, however, is the preference of people who would use the expressway once built but would prefer that it were not built.

In any case, there are not many objective measures of behavior projectible to a regional, county, or even local plan.

Providing a Framework for Wide Choice—If no method of infusing people's desires into land-use plans seems likely to work, perhaps the best course is a plan which maximizes choice. We may not be able to tell in advance whether the coming generation will prefer high density or low, urban experience or arm's length from each other, but we can insure that there is a range of options open to them. We could build some urban regions that are city oriented—e.g., New York, San Francisco, Atlanta, Minneapolis—and some spread city, e.g., Los Angeles, Detroit. Within each region, we could provide a wide choice of densities and housing types. Within the city-oriented regions, we could have small centers as well as large, low-density communities as well as medium and high. Of course this plan may not fit future preferences perfectly. It may not provide enough of one or another kind of environment. Furthermore, to achieve variety rather than a continuation of spread city everywhere will require a strong commitment to new public policies and controls—and this will require broad public support. So the issue of public participation cannot, after all, be avoided.

DIRECT PUBLIC PARTICIPATION IN PLANNING

How to Involve the Public—Regional Plan Association's experience and self-examination after more than a decade of public participation experiments suggest the following principles:

1. To get useful responses on these issues from the public, considerable information and ideas must be presented to the public.
   a. A market research doorstep poll is inadequate because the sum of personal preferences is unlikely to be a workable plan for a whole area. Most persons' individual preferences usually are in conflict, let alone the preferences of all the persons whose environment is created at once. Furthermore, they may not be familiar with the options available.
   b. A completely open series of meetings in which participants are asked to start the discussion themselves with their own problems and hopes and preferences may be useful but is not sufficient. The important questions relate to future problems, about which most persons must learn from planners' projections. For example, Regional Plan's public participation efforts began in a period of euphoria—the early 1960s. Those who had recently moved out of the older cities particularly seemed to feel they had found the ultimate in urban living, and the old cities were not yet seen to be in a declining spiral. Indeed New York City had been having a housing boom.

      Yet the seeds of the horrendous decade we have just lived through had long since been planted—the cities' decay, deprivation of opportunities for the poor, a rapidly-growing housing gap, a widening chasm between black and white, and the resulting social tensions. Their eventual fruit was visible to the Association. In 1963, the Regional Plan presentation dragged participants reluctantly and often angrily into facing the future. Without that, a get-together of typical New York Region residents would never have dealt with reality. The same situation with an opposite twist would be true today. The past decade is still too much with us—the riots, the welfare boom, the crime wave, small groups stopping the whole machinery of society, a sharp decline in city services, the sudden recognition that we are poisoning ourselves with our wastes and running through world resources profligately. Our emotional state has not begun to respond to the fact that none of the negative social forces ever did move to its logical conclusion, that all of them have begun to come under better control, that U. S. population growth has slowed almost to a halt with the end in sight, and that the energy shortage, if faced squarely, can force us to create what we might well have chosen but would otherwise never have organized ourselves to attain. In short, without a longer-term view of today's conditions, we might err on the side of fear today as we did in the direction of self-satisfaction in 1963.

2. Regional Plan's method of relating to the public has four parts: (a) written material in advance, (b) audio-visual presentation of the same concepts as appeared in print, (c) discussion by all participants in small groups to test their ideas and share information, and (d) individual response on written questionnaires. Each of these parts contributes something different and important.

3. The process is aimed not only at telling planners what people think of their concepts but also at informing the public so they can take part effectively in land-use decisions as the decisions are made by government. And it encourages them to do so.

4. We do not check the technical competence of the planning and research in this process. (That is done regularly on professional colleagues in related agencies.) We test our assumptions—and we do it as we go along in the research: first the projections of things to come if present trends and policies continue; then alternative patterns of land use and their resulting life styles; finally, the kind of public policy and institutional changes needed to achieve the preferred alternatives.

People seldom have time to examine the dozens of assumptions on which their everyday decisions are based. But they should take time when making long-range decisions. By the time planners get through piling data on their assumptions about what people worry about and want, the assumptions are almost invisible. They should be unearthed and examined. An illustration: a regional planning commission was considering a huge expressway program. The commission—representing the public—was impressed with the sophisticated study that had been done by the planning staff. The commission spent most of the day going over the technical process of how the staff arrived at its recommended highway network. It was not until late in the day that one commissioner asked the kind of question the commission should have started with: "What average speed is this system designed for during rush hours?" "Thirty-five miles an hour." "What would the system be like if it were designed for an average speed of, say, 32 miles per hour?" The difference was millions of dollars and a good deal less disruption. Now that is the kind of question the public should ask of the planners, and the public's answer on that kind of question should have strong influence. This innocent-sounding query led to another hidden assumption: the staff had assumed that anyone in this metropolitan area should be able to live on one side and work on the other and get to work by car in what they had assumed to be a "reasonable" time.

While this is a strikingly clear example, it is by no means unusual in the point it illustrates. Five years ago, for example, the Port Authority of New York and New Jersey got the region debating whether to build a fourth major jetport, solely on the argument that travel demand would soon exceed air space. Like any good purveyor of services, the Port Authority assumed that it should provide any services the customer demands. The public was not told that the billion-dollar ten-square-mile project would buy only the right of a relative handful of people to arrive and leave exactly when they wanted whether by small private plane or by giant airliner, each with equal access to the scarce airspace.

Planners, then, must be encouraged to unearth the assumptions on which the huge superstructure of their data-laden analyses are based, and the public should be educated to look for them.

5. There are a number of difficulties in interpreting the public's response.

   a. Typically, the well-educated, middle-aged and upper-middle-income show up when discussions of planning issues are announced. It takes special approaches and perhaps specially-organized meetings to involve adequate numbers of those without college education.

   b. Furthermore, those who take part vary in their ability to understand the issues and to imagine how they would react to various conditions. And we are asking them for an even greater act of imagination—projecting themselves into conditions they have never seen, let alone experienced.

   c. Some people care far more about these land-use issues than others. Should all opinions count the same?

These hurdles do not prevent effective public impact on land use, but they do require that the results of public involvement be interpreted in their light. A reassuring factor is that the mere anticipation that different groups of people may be listening and responding is bound to make planners try to look at their work from the vantage point of the various groups that might be participating. "How will blacks see this? How department store executives? How factory workers? How residents of X county?"

It would seem possible to find spokesmen who would accurately reflect the views of groups who do not participate in civic affairs—spokesmen who could be cajoled to sit still long enough to consider the issues carefully, perhaps just a few people across the table from someone who can explain the issues and background orally. These should not be civic leaders (e.g., the local NAACP leader or minister or priest) but bartenders, union shop stewards, social workers, credit-union clerks—people in a position to hear what nonrepresented kinds of people think but who do not consider themselves their leaders on these kinds of issues. This is important because in sociological studies and Regional Plan experience it has been shown that leaders do not always have the same views as those for whom they speak. For example, in a recent Regional Plan project, black leaders objected to asking the public whether the U. S. should try to induce jobs to leave the Region in order to lower population growth there. Poor people, they argued, would not have enough money to follow their jobs out of the Region. Instead of dropping the question, Regional Plan included that argument against favoring the proposal. Black and Puerto Rican respondents *favored* exporting jobs out of the Region even more than others. Similarly, we added a statement reflecting black spokesmen's views that blacks should stay in the older cities to enhance their political strength; but black voters were strongly for integration, for more suburban housing opportunities, and for keeping older cities the centers of activities for whites and blacks both.

Special Considerations in Regional Planning—The size of most urban regions in the United States, the complexity of the planning issues, and the paucity of talent in presenting these issues seem to us to necessitate the use of mass media for conveying the essential information to those who will participate in regional planning.

Regional Plan Association has twice used a series of television programs to present regional planning issues, along with background reading. Citizen groups were organized to discuss the issues. Finally, written questionnaires were widely distributed. In the more recent project, CHOICES FOR '76 conducted in March, April, and May, 1973, an average of 26,500 ballots were returned for each of five regional "town meetings." (A full evaluation of the project is available from Regional Plan Association.) Because so many people took part, there were enough ballots from lower-income people, blacks, and those without a college education so that their opinions as well as those of the college educated white higher-income people could be known. In addition, George Gallup's organization tested on a scientific sample of the New York Region 11 of the 51 questions asked and found that there was no special tendency of CHOICES participants that would make their opinions significantly different from the public as a whole. However, watching the television (as about 70 percent of the balloters did) and reading the background book, *How To Save Urban America* (as over 10 percent did), strongly affected responses on nearly all of the questions.

It is important to see that this participation process was part of a whole series of public testing of regional planning concepts over more than a dozen years of evolving a plan for the New York Region. Meetings with carefully selected advisory groups, special interest groups, and broad civic-interest organizations took place constantly as the research was being done and the ideas formulated. So the television town meeting project was essentially to test on the broadest possible public an already well-tested set of proposed solutions to carefully researched problems of the Region.

The responses to CHOICES questions showed the region's civic and political leaders which new policies were well-received when the public saw them in the context of a broad plan. For example, they showed that a substantial majority favored statewide school taxes, which most political leaders have not dared to advance; and operating subsidies for public transportation were almost unanimously supported. It also gave one part of the region a chance to express an opinion on issues now decided only by another part—such as housing location. A majority of city residents favored a change in suburban zoning to allow more privately financed housing that middle-income families could afford; the older suburbs, with little vacant land, slightly favored the change; but the outer suburbs, where the zoning is in question, were clearly opposed. State legislators from city constituencies might find this a worthwhile crusade.

Regional Plan is now proposing a continuing series of television programs on more specific pending issues. The programs would show the regional planning context of each issue, present the arguments on both sides, and explain how the public can have a voice—i.e., which governmental unit is to make the decision. This is designed to keep those who took part in CHOICES continually involved.

In sum, at the regional level, planners must continually test their ideas on as broad a set of diverse interests as possible and then inform as large a public as possible of the regional planning implications of day-to-day decisions being made by governments at all levels. City residents must know how suburban zoning affects them—and how to have a voice in the decisions; conservationists must know that where facilities should go is as important as where they should not go in ultimate saving of open land; those concerned with broadening employment opportunities for lower-income people must recognize the importance of where the jobs and education opportunities locate and of transportation.

Participation in National Development Policies—Are nationally televised town meetings needed to set national development policies? They might be very valuable, but they would be extremely difficult. Generalizing to cover conditions in the whole New York Region was hard in CHOICES FOR '76; generalizing so people everywhere in the country could see their involvement would be ten times harder. And a nationally televised town meeting probably would not be necessary. If urban regions throughout the country developed plans on the basis of widespread public participation, the national issues affecting land use would be opened to scrutiny: where not to build—state and federal development limitations and national parks; federal welfare standards and other anti-poverty spending; which parts of the country should get federal contracts and other development incentives; whether federal installations should conform to regional plans; and federal transportation policies and priorities. Congressional debate on these issues might be sufficient public involvement after the people in each urban region had become acquainted with the effect of national decisions on their regional plans.

Well, What Do People Want?

We have concentrated on how to find out public land-use preferences because very little is known about what people really want. Several public opinion surveys have been made, but—as we have said—they cannot be relied on by themselves. Interviewees did not know the full range of options or all the costs of their choices—social and ecological as well as personal. Nevertheless, these surveys can provide guidance to the planner who puts together policy choices for public response.

INDIVIDUAL PREFERENCES REVEALED IN POLLS

A minor and declining share of recently polled Americans would choose to live in large cities, but a majority continues to want the benefits of the city—a wide choice of jobs and services—and so would choose to live within 30 miles of a city of over 50,000, but in smaller cities, small towns, or rural areas. Several polls taken in the late 1960s and early 1970s support this conclusion. To put numbers on it, a 1972 national survey showed 25 percent preferred to live in a city of over 50,000; 55 percent within 30 miles of such a city but not in it; 19 percent in a smaller city, town, or rural area outside the range of a large city. Several surveys indicate that crime and air quality—rather than density—are among the main reasons an increasing number choose to leave the cities.[2]

This preference for trying to get the best of both the urban and the rural or small town world has been demonstrated in housing choices actually made in many urban regions over the past decade or two. But since so many people are trying to do the same thing—tack onto an urban area at the rural fringe—not many succeed. The result has been the spread city, which is not the best of the urban and rural—it may be the worst. The situation has bred one of the continuing conflicts of urban planning —the new suburbanite trying to stop the outward population flow as soon as he has flowed out.

A different kind of study, on housing demand, showed that people generally prefer more indoor and outdoor space than they have, and a great majority want one family houses. But it also shows that people generally will remain in their present neighborhood despite preferences for more space if the neighborhood quality is not disturbed. The study also found that when housing costs exceed a family's financial capacity, they would cut back first on the yard size they aspire to. Privacy more than spaciousness seems to be what is desired, both indoors and outdoors.[3]

Children, of course, affect housing and area choice. Along with crime

2 Glenn V. Fuguitt and James J. Zuiches, "Residential Preferences and Population Distribution," Mimeo paper, August 29, 1973.

3 Joint Center for Urban Studies, Massachusetts Institute of Technology and Harvard University, "America's Housing Needs: 1970–1980," December, 1973.

and air pollution, "better for the children" is the most frequently given reason for preferring an out-of-city residence; and the housing study found that "high status" people seek out suburbs where school quality is emphasized if they have children; if not, they tend to choose either inner city neighborhoods or exurbia. So the rapid increase in households without school-age children will affect housing demand and urban development patterns.

While social conditions (crime and school integration) have led to greater suburbanization and spreading out, better design may be leading toward more compact housing. A recent survey by the Urban Land Institute suggests a growing preference for attached houses, particularly if well designed and built. Of a sample of present town house dwellers, 42 percent plan to stay for at least five years. While two-thirds of town house residents in the East are biding their time until they can afford a one-family house, three-fourths of those living in the West chose town houses because maintenance is easier; and three-eighths chose them because of recreational facilities. They have selected—not settled for—attached housing. Nevertheless, even town house dwellers indicate preference for moderate densities (four to ten units per acre) rather than higher. That preference is modified by design and by what is around the project: looking just at half of the projects rated most satisfactory by residents, a fifth were 10 units to the acre or denser.[4]

GOALS FOR DALLAS

Because individual preferences do conflict and often ignore the trade-offs, the few examples of public participation in land-use policy-making seem to us to provide more relevant views.

The only large public participation effort comparable in scope to Regional Plan's CHOICES FOR '76 is Goals for Dallas; well over 50,000 people took part. This project began by considering generalized goals, mainly for the city but including the Dallas-Fort Worth urban region in some of its recommendations. Background papers helped to initiate discussion. It was done in face-to-face groups, without television.

Only a few of the issues dealt with land use. On these, the conclusions were:

—Continue to foster economic growth in the city and region.
—Design the central business district as a multi-purpose area for commercial, governmental, educational, cultural, recreational and residential use. Growth of the resident downtown population will stimulate life and growth in the other uses.
—Consider subsidizing public transit by the metropolitan region.

[4] Carl Norcross, *Townhouses and Condominiums,* Urban Land Institute, 1973.

CHOICES FOR '76 AND OTHER REGIONAL PLAN ASSOCIATION SURVEYS

Regional Plan opinion surveys concentrated on land-use policies. The results of 11 projects over the last decade are summarized here: a regional conference in 1968 with 500 questionnaire returns, eight subsequent county conferences with 1,900 returns in all, CHOICES FOR '76 described above, and Goals for the Region—a project similar to CHOICES but on a much smaller scale (an average of about 4,200 returns from each of five sessions) in 1963.

Regional Population Growth—Unlike Dallas citizens, a majority of CHOICES participants in all demographic groups opposed job and population growth. To do that, they were willing to support more extensive birth control and abortion measures (67%–21%) and federal incentives to move jobs out of the region in order to slow population growth (59–25). This was a new attitude. In all but two of the previous Regional Plan opinion surveys, a majority opposed efforts to induce jobs out of the Region.

The main difference that can explain the change in opinion is what participants knew about the probable effects of growth. In CHOICES, questions on whether to allow the Region to grow came up before the possibilities for accommodating expected growth had been made clear. In other presentations, how growth could be accommodated satisfactorily was thoroughly discussed before questions were asked on whether to allow growth. Nevertheless, the feeling against growth among CHOICES participants was strong; the remedies they voted to accept were not portrayed as easy.

Centers and Communities—There was substantial support for the idea of keeping the development that does take place in the Region focused on urban centers—particularly by renewing and enlarging old downtowns. Eight out of ten in CHOICES called for rebuilding older cities as major centers of economic activity and housing, with only 6 percent feeling that old cities should become primarily residential areas for minorities and only 3 percent favoring the abandonment of the old cities over time. Twelve percent of black voters and 17 percent of Puerto Ricans favored letting cities become primarily residential areas for minorities.

Where no older downtown exists, new downtowns should be built rather than dispersing major activities, according to 70 percent; 18 percent disagreed.

But when it came to specifics, some respondents did not follow through. Asked about office locations, many more respondents preferred that they be in old downtowns (66–16) and new downtowns (48–27) than along highways or on campus sites (26–45), but nowhere near the percentages favoring downtowns in theory. Similarly with the idea that housing should relate to the center, with highest density in and near the center, tapering off to lower density. That was approved almost 2–1 among those who gave an answer, but more than a quarter of the respondents did not feel qualified to express an opinion. Those who watched the TV program or read the background book voted more than 20 points higher than those who did not, which is understandable with such a sophisticated concept.

Participants also approved, by about 2–1, "complete residential communities with mixed housing types and price ranges on vacant land, in lieu of traditional subdivisions."

And a related concept: participants favored state action to achieve *compact* urban development 52–31 over *spread* urban development. Again, the concept was sophisticated, and TV viewers and background book readers viewed it far more favorably than voters who indicated they had done neither. Support for compact development went up with increased income and education. The poorest and least educated were much more undecided and split evenly for and against.

Support for the centers-and-communities concept and for a more compact walking and public transportation Region was much stronger and more consistent in previous Regional Plan surveys. Differences in the wording of the question could have explained the greater consistency. Also more education and a much higher percentage of the participants reading the book and seeing the full audio-visual presentation certainly added to the support and the consistency of opinions in the earlier Regional Plan programs. Finally, having the presentation in one day and face-to-face rather than over an eight-week period on television, as in CHOICES, undoubtedly strengthened comprehension.

Earlier surveys gave a choice of large or small centers. In 1963, a majority of Goals for the Region respondents favored smaller over large centers (50–34); in 1968, when Regional Plan's theory of centers was more developed, the vote was 49–46 for large centers. Subsequent county meeting responses were even more in favor of large centers, usually specifically related to their own areas.

Housing—All participants strongly favored a statewide school tax, presented as a necessary first step to getting more new unsubsidized housing. It would eliminate the tax burden that would result from rezoning for houses which can be built more inexpensively than the one-family homes on large lots that are now almost exclusively required on vacant land.

But when it came to whether the zoning should be changed to get more attached housing and homes on small lots—"even if some zoning responsibility were shifted to county or state government" to achieve that—the CHOICES vote was only 48–44. However, those who read the book and watched the TV programs were 35 points more in favor than those who did not. It is noted above that city residents supported this zoning change and outer suburbanites opposed. A similar difference was revealed on allowing more mobile home parks, except that even the outer areas had slight pluralities in favor and the city residents provided considerably smaller majorities.

In earlier Regional Plan surveys—even in the suburban and exurban counties, there was strong support for county and state veto of local zoning if needed to get more housing.

CHOICES participants were evenly split on whether low-income public housing should go in or out of the ghetto (a majority of blacks were in favor of putting it outside). Support for more public housing was 71–16. In earlier surveys, there was support for building public housing out of the ghetto. The difference in voting may be explained as above: earlier participants had on the average much more education and at least half read the book, compared to one in eight of CHOICES respondents. Almost all saw an audio-visual presentation compared to less than three-fourths of CHOICES participants seeing the film. And the whole concept of regional development was presented live at once rather than in pieces on TV over an eight-week period.

In the 1963 Goals project, we asked some of the questions in a more personal way, e.g., how would you feel about low income housing developments in your community? If they were garden apartments, support was 60–24; higher apartments aroused majority opposition. Looking at a smaller, closer-to-home area we called a neighborhood, we asked participants to list all the social situations they would "like." A majority said they liked living in a neighborhood with people of the same income and race as themselves, and almost a majority said they liked living with *either* a different race *or* a different income group but not both a different race and income. We interpreted this to mean that the predominantly white upper-middle-income sample did not mind low-income white or higher-income blacks but did not want to live near low-income blacks. The Joint Center for Urban Studies housing study noted above reported a similar response in a survey in Boston—60 percent favored social variety in their neighborhood but not lower class and not too wide a social span.

Because there are so many variables affecting housing preferences—income, number of children and their ages, where a person already lives, and even religion (Jews preferred apartments in greater numbers than non-Jews) and because our 1963 sample was so biased in all of these regards, we compared what people liked in housing with what they had. Generally we found about a quarter liked living in apartments (they perhaps liked living in a one-family house, too), and about the same percentage did live in apartments (though not the same quarter). About 10 percent of the rest who were living in one-family houses preferred somewhat larger lots than they were living on.

Of those with children under six, 35 percent lived in apartments and only 21 percent liked living in apartments, while of those with school-age children, only 8 percent lived in apartments and 16 percent liked apartment living.

Dislike of living on smaller than half-acre lots went up with income. Two-thirds of those having incomes below $7,000 liked smaller than half-acre lots, while only half of those with incomes around $10,000 and slightly less than half of higher-income families liked the idea.

Some 13 percent of all participants liked garden apartments; 9 percent high-rise. More high-income families—even with children—liked high-rise apartments than the sample as a whole.

But in surveys from 1968–1972, more than 2.5 times as many respondents said they would choose to live in an apartment or town house if there were a center to which the apartments related than if there were a spread-city pattern—more than a third would choose attached housing units if there were a center. And only about two-thirds as many would choose a half-acre lot or larger if there were centers compared to spread city—less than a quarter of the respondents requiring such a large lot if there were centers.

A bare majority of CHOICES participants (in 1973) favored subsidizing housing to keep middle-income families living in cities, and there was little difference in the votes demographically. Much higher percentages of earlier project participants had favored this.

Transportation—In all Regional Plan surveys, 1963 through 1973, greater reliance on public transportation has been favored almost unanimously. A majority of CHOICES respondents was willing to take two steps needed for good transit: (1) cluster the higher density buildings (mainly apartments and offices) near transit stops (58–26) and (2) subsidize transit (83–14). (Then why the defeat of two recent bond issues in New York State? Perhaps the share of funds to be applied to highways, perhaps the "credibility gap" in politics these days.) A further step needed— higher residential densities than we have been building recently—received a bare 43–40 plurality. On both of the density issues, watching TV and reading the book made a huge difference in response, as did more education.

Only 22 percent of CHOICES voters wanted to stop expressway construction and another 19 percent wanted to slow construction compared to 55 percent who wanted to build expressways at least as fast as we were doing. Support for more expressways went down as income and education went up, and young people were much more for them than their elders. A large majority of all groups felt the new expressways should be in developed areas now poorly served by highways rather than in outer areas scarcely inhabited. City people were no more opposed to expressways than others.

On earlier surveys, Regional Plan found much stronger opposition to highways. Over a four-year period, participants were asked to respond to the statement: "Limiting the number of new expressways in the Region to protect the environment is more important right now than enlarging opportunities for fast auto travel by building more highways." Agreement varied from county to county from over 5–1 in Westchester to just over 2–1 in Middlesex County, New Jersey, with the 3.5–1 of the Region-wide conference about average. In part, the greater opposition to highway building on earlier projects compared to CHOICES is attributable to the higher education and income of participants. Or again, it may have been the opportunity in before-CHOICES projects to see the whole plan in one sitting. The CHOICES book and television presentation dealt with the issue of expressway construction far more thoroughly than previous Association projects, but that does not seem to have been the reason for the vote difference. Those who read the CHOICES book and watched television were *more* opposed than other CHOICES voters to continuing rapid expressway construction; and so if the presentation had any effect, it brought CHOICES people *more* in line with previous project participants rather than less.

Parks—CHOICES participants were decisively in favor of cluster zoning to leave some public open space in new or renewed neighborhoods (66–22). All demographic groups were more favorable than opposed.

As to large public open tracts, a majority supported the idea of buying now all the open space that would be needed for the next half century (54–29). All groups provided majority support except those with incomes under $4,000 (49 percent), those under 21, and blacks and Puerto Ricans (44 percent). On earlier surveys, the vote was far more decisive, e.g., 82–5 in the regional meeting. As to where the parks should be: for city people, they should be in the cities primarily—rather than large, distant parks with inexpensive travel to them (79–16 with all demographic groups favoring).

Summary of Opinions—Generalizing, it seems that these more educated than average predominantly white suburbanite civic activists, when exposed to written and audio-visual information about urban options, want to go back to the old form of downtowns, compact cities, somewhat more spacious but not sprawling suburbs, all tied together by good public transportation with open space in each neighborhood and substantial public open space outside. With such a pattern, about half would be willing to live at higher densities than they otherwise would choose, well over a third saying they would live in an apartment or town house to be near a vibrant urban center.

While there is clearly a resistance among white respondents to living near low-income blacks, there is recognition (expressed on several questions) that segregation is unsatisfactory for both blacks and whites. There is support for rebuilding older cities to satisfy middle-income families in order to achieve integration—particularly new towns in town with more open space and play areas than present cities have. There is less support for opening the suburbs to low-income families.

In short, the vote is fairly substantial—among these people and under these conditions—against spread city.

Then Why Are We Building Spread City?—Each person and institution planning by itself finds that his immediate situation favors spread city. Centers-and-communities cannot offer its advantages unless the pattern is followed by almost everyone in an urban region. And without clear land-use policies—incentives to attract and controls to keep the recalcitrant from going in a different direction—the concerted action required to achieve centers-and-communities cannot be attained. We shall simply continue to build spread city.

TO ACHIEVE WHAT PEOPLE HAVE SAID THEY WANT

The kind of land-use policies people have chosen after receiving the necessary information and being encouraged to discuss them will require redistribution of authority to those strongly affected: some authority to the whole urban region (perhaps through state governments for a time), some to metropolitan communities within the regions (perhaps through county governments for now), while other controls remain with the localities.

We need more extensive experiments with public participation in the planning process. More of the public is eager to take part, but the machinery and skills must be improved.

When we make land-use decisions piecemeal without an over-all conception of the kind of place we want to live in, as we are doing now, we cannot but decide primarily how to avoid the worst. But if we get together, all those concerned enough to plan the future, this wealthiest nation in world history with the highest degree of education and the most leisure to dispose of, surely can contemplate instead the building of a great civilization. And with appropriate incentives and land-use controls, we can build it.

Donald G. Hagman

5

Windfalls for Wipeouts

Introduction

Governments build public works projects and enact regulations. In the wake of such activity, some property owners are fortuitously visited with enormous increases in land value—they are the windfallers. Meanwhile, and equally by chance, other landowners suffer substantial losses in value—they are wiped out by governmental activity.

Consider landowner Jones who bought a parcel of property in 1965 for $5,000. In 1973 a station for a new subway is located on adjacent property, and the city rezones his property from single-family to multiple-family high-rise. Without his lifting a finger, Jones' property may now be worth $500,000.

Meanwhile, consider landowner Smith, who bought a similar parcel in 1965 for $5,000. The city acquires an adjacent parcel for a garbage incinerator and subsequently, having discovered that Smith's land is a habitat for a rare insect, rezones his land from single-family residential to a conservancy district, which leaves Smith with virtually no use of his property. Smith's property is now worth $500.

Would it be fairer to devise mechanisms for recapturing Jones' windfall in part in order to mitigate Smith's wipeout? It might be prudent to devise those mechanisms soon, for (1) the tough environmental regulation of recent years has (2) magnified the inequity problem and led to other counterproductive behavior; and (3) those who have been visited with disproportionate burdens in the name of a better environment are striking back, with justice as their clarion call.

Author of numerous books and articles on planning, land use, environment, state and local taxation, and local government, DONALD G. HAGMAN *is Professor of Law at The University of California (Los Angeles).*

Tough New Environmental Regulation

FEDERAL

On December 31, 1969, *federal* regulation of private land use was virtually non-existent. But the birthday of the decade and of the National Environmental Policy Act (NEPA) coincided. NEPA has been the environmental workhorse—stopping, delaying, and changing proposed land uses.

The nation celebrated NEPA's first birthday by giving it a companion environmental juggernaut—the Clean Air Amendments of 1970. Among other things, the Act required states to prepare implementation plans indicating how they intended to meet the requirements of the Act, which provided that air would be of a certain quality throughout America by a certain date. The words of land use note were that, if necessary to attain or maintain clean air, implementation plans had to include "land-use and transportation controls."

As the Environmental Protection Agency (EPA) implemented the Act through its transportation and so-called "indirect" source rules, it became apparent in late 1973 that the entire pattern of consumptive, sprawling, automobile-based land use was to be massively reversed in metropolitan areas almost overnight. Fortuitously or not, the energy crisis of 1974 nipped implementation in the bud, though curiously, energy saving initiatives have many of the same land-use effects as the EPA regulations.

It took a bit longer for the federal water pollution fraternity to muscle in on the land-use control act. After all, the Water Pollution Control Act Amendments of 1972 had to be passed over a Presidential veto, not an easy task on October 18, 1972, when the Water Act became law. The EPA also administers that Act. The effects are that private sources of pollution must locate other than where water is polluted, moratoria on development are required wherever in the country public sewer systems are inadequate, land uses that cause pollution by runoff are banned in areas of poor water quality, and sewer construction grants that subsidize sprawl are ended.

The Noise Control Act of 1972 has land-use implications on location of airports, railroad yards, and the like. And the Flood Disaster Prevention Act of 1973 all but eliminates the possibility of building in flood-prone areas.

The Coastal Zone Management Act of 1972 is more of an aid to planning than it is a federal take-over of land-use control. And even if so-called national land-use planning came in the form of the Land Use Policy and Planning Assistance Act (LUPPAA), such legislation would again basically be planning aid. It might help subnational governments to put together federal land-use control which comes in through the back door under NEPA and the pollution laws—laws which were largely uncoordinated with one another and which in combination reacted violently to produce idiosyncratic impacts on land use.

STATE AND LOCAL

The substantial federal inroads over the control of land use did not displace other controls. State and regional land-use control was *the* hot land-use topic of the early 70s. As distinguished from the federal story, the state and regional story has been told, for example, by Bosselman and Callies in the *Quiet Revolution in Land Use Control,* a frequently cited book. These pages afford no space to retell the story. Nor do these pages permit the retelling of how individual localities in various states have acted, whether or not the states have acted. Managed growth policies have given new fame to Petaluma, California; Boca Raton, Florida; Ramapo, New York; Boulder, Colorado; and hundreds of other communities. So it is from sea to polluted sea.

Growing Magnitude of Windfalls and Wipeouts

All these tough new federal, state, regional, and local regulations have magnified the windfall and wipeout problem. Demand for land, after all, is relatively constant; indeed, with a growing and increasingly affluent population, we are becoming a more land consumptive society. As this demand seeks a supply, it is directed away from some locations and to other locations by regulation—only weak zoning regulations in yesteryear—from the new environmental juggernauts today. Landowners in developable locations have a windfall; those heavily restricted suffer heavy wipeouts.

One should also remember that the multiplicity and complexity of the hurdles have an important bearing on both the severity and magnitude of windfalls and wipeouts. In yesteryear, development was possible either by way of right or by a rezoning that was easily obtained by a local small builder from his friendly real-estate-industry-dominated city council. Since development permission was easily obtained, those that were obtained included little windfall.

Compare that with today. In order to get development permission, a developer may need to deal directly or indirectly with four levels of government—local, regional, state, and federal; with several specialized agencies each dealing with less than all of the traditional land-use controls (e.g., zoning, subdivision, subdivided lands, official map, grading, building permit laws); with one or more agencies each to consider air, water, and noise pollution; in many states with local environmental impact statements and perhaps with NEPA requirements. Many of these laws are new, complex, being enacted with machine-gun rapidity, and since many of the laws exist in splendid isolation from one another, the result of being foisted on various levels of government by environmental zealots of different messianic beliefs, there is no synergistic effect. Understanding one law does not mean that one understands another. And there is no domino effect. Getting a permit from one agency for one aspect of development does not mean that the next agency will give its permit. In fact, since environmentalists and the like want to oppose more than their resources will permit, effective opposition to projects in their early stages is unlikely. Things slip through; the cry of alarm goes out at the last moment, and the last public decision-maker is visited with the omniscient and often omnipotent omnipresence of citizen participants, who clothe their special interests with the public interest.

Who has the staying power and intelligence to deal with these hurdles? Not even a relatively large-scale corporate developer can do so. The ability to accept risk, the waiting power to deal with delay, the wisdom to hire specialists with knowledge to understand the complexity of laws is not even there. The capability may exist only with the large-scale multinational conglomerate—those who are highly sophisticated, diversified, and capitalized. They and only they can risk the wipeout; they and only they can reap the windfall. Those who can get that final permission and become suppliers of developed land have a virtual monopoly because so few suppliers can jump all the hurdles. The demand focuses on that supply, and presto—a windfall.

Unless we are extremely Darwinian about it, we should be concerned for those poor slobs and enterprises which have not evolved to be able to deal with the new environmentalism. For example, it may affect the poor widow who had hung onto her husband's legacy, a chunk of real estate, which she had hoped to sell in order to send her child to college. She cannot gamble on a windfall because she cannot risk the wipeout. Governments now roll their environmental regulatory juggernauts across the landscape with no institutions having a whit of a care that some gain monopoly profits while others lose lifetime investments. Perhaps we should care on equity grounds.

Windfalls and Wipeouts: Counterproductive Effects

RESISTANCE TO ENVIRONMENTALISM

Moreover, the wipeout problem affects the very continuation of the environmental movement. The poor widow will not support it. The developer in Boca Raton, Florida, whose partially completed project is reduced from 150 to 18 units per acre as a result of the city's "dwelling unit cap" will not ho-hum his way to bankruptcy. Such persons, and investors and labor union members, will band together, as they have in Orange County, California, to try to qualify "The People's Initiative to

Protect Property Rights" as an amendment to the California constitution. The initiative reads:

> No interest in . . . property . . . shall be . . . damaged or diminished in value for public use, benefit or convenience, under the police [regulatory] power or otherwise, unless full and just compensation is made. . . .

These persons will also clog the courts with lawsuits, like those now filed around the country, with claims for damages amounting to billions of dollars.

PERCEIVED ARBITRARINESS

Persons suffering wipeouts especially cannot be expected to be sanguine in the face of a neighbor's windfall. The myth that some brooding omni-planning in the sky justifies some persons getting the goodies while others are deprived cannot explain away the harsh and fiscally substantial reality that who gets the goodies is essentially arbitrary and capricious. When windfalls and wipeouts were small, a planners' explanation of why A got permission to develop while B did not was likely to be accepted. When the stakes are higher, the explanations are examined more carefully and largely found wanting.

Furthermore, respect for law diminishes when there is great irrationality and berserk line-drawing between regulation without compensation and eminent domain with compensation, though both may be equally severe. Deciding on when compensation should be paid and when not is the hardest issue in land-use control law, and the law is in a grand state of disarray. Responsible voices have urged that no compensation should be paid if a government decides to effectuate environmental goals by regulation, regardless of the impact that regulation has on individual land-owners.[1] Payment should be made, they argue, only if a government decides to use eminent domain or to be more generous than the constitution requires and pay compensation when regulation "takes" a large bite of value from property. Can the city council of Smallsville be assumed to make that decision responsibly? I think not. A rule which bases the necessity for compensation on the *means* used by government is simple, but it may not produce fairness. A fairer rule would be: whenever government acts in the public interest, and however it acts, when that interest is served at the great expense of a limited number of private property owners, some compensation should be paid. But there is a correlative rule— whenever a limited number of private property owners capture govern-mentally created benefits, part of the monetary value of those benefits should be recaptured for the public.

---

[1] F. Bosselman, D. Callies & J. Banta, *The Taking Issue* (1973); Citizens' Advisory Committee on Environmental Quality Task Force on Land Use and Urban Growth, *The Use of Land* (1973).

Such rules would be regarded as fairer, respect for law would be enhanced, environmental initiatives would face less resistance, and government could use an appropriate means rather than a means cleverly bent beyond recognition simply because it is cheap. Movement in the direction of such results is the purpose of anti-wipeout, windfall recapture techniques.

CORRUPTION

The present system, since it incorporates few such techniques, corrupts government. When great windfalls or wipeouts are possible and government acts with considerable discretion, as it generally does in exercising land-use controls, there are considerable funds available for campaign financing or more direct payoffs. Consider an example of which there are now hundreds in America. A developer acquires land and begins its development only to have a moratorium on development laid on by a five-man city council in a rather small community. The developer's total investment translates to carrying costs of say $5,000 per day or $150,000 per month. (I have heard of cases where carrying costs were $20,000 per day.) If three councilmen could be persuaded to accept a bribe, the developer could afford to pay each of them $50,000, probably double their annual income, and be out of pocket only what it costs to carry the project under the moratorium for one month. The temptation to bribery is overwhelming, and too many developers and local government officials have yielded to the temptation. Of course, innumerable more have used such funds to find and support more sympathetic candidates in local elections.

If one considered all functions of government, and then did a study to determine how much graft or campaign contributions were attributable to each function, the land-use control function would surely rank high on the list. At the local level, where most land-use controls are still exercised, land-use decisions provide the main opportunity for local government corruption because the exercise of these controls unlocks the largest windfalls and wipeouts. Under an anti-wipeout, windfall-recapture system, the stakes are reduced and the amount of funds available for corruption are lessened.

UNDUE SPECIAL INTEREST

Studies have indicated that the local real estate industry is often generously represented on boards of appeal, planning commissions, and city councils, particularly in communities undergoing development or redevelopment. Of course, some representation from that industry is appropriate. The people in it are knowledgeable. But the interest of persons from that industry serving local government is often indecently keen. Generally, pay is non-existent or minimal for part-time elective or appointive jobs. But opportunities abound. One's own or one's friend's chance to gain windfalls or to avoid wipeouts are not always sharply distinguishable from the public interest. An anti-wipeout, windfall-recapture system would tend to reduce the incentive to clothe the public interest with one's own interest.

NO PLANNING

The present system, of course, does not produce much attention to the public interest in any event. The reason is that most land-use control decisions give rise to only neighborhood externalities. Neighbor is fighting neighbor. There being no other mechanism for resolving the externality problem, and yet the public decision unleashing private impacts, the private impacts are considered by the governmental decision makers. Exhausted by the private concerns, there is no time or energy left to care for the public interest.

An example may help. A multi-family developer buys a lot on the fringes of a single-family home subdivision. He seeks a rezoning of the area to permit that use. Two hundred neighbors petition and most appear before the planning commission and the city council. All those voters being present, no public servant is gutsy enough to give less than all of them their day in "court." The result is either that the rezoning is denied, despite the fact that it may be in the larger public interest that it be granted, or that the decision-making body spends all of its time working out a "deal"—larger sideyards, multiple-family housing built to look like single-family housing, larger, more costly, fewer units so as to raise the likely socio-economic characteristics of the potential occupants of the multiple-family housing, etc. Meanwhile, the other decisions on the agenda are put off to another meeting—decisions such as approving the general plan, or considering a comprehensive revision of the zoning ordinance. Somehow, these larger public questions—harder, often duller, and thought-demanding—do not get made, or get made at the staff level. The excitement, the action, the emotion is in the fray. It is another sad example of how administration swallows up policy formulation.

Under an anti-wipeout, windfall-recapture system, the multiple-family developer might be required to pay-off the neighbors up to the amount of his windfall, limited by the amount of the externality (wipeout). That might dissuade some of the neighbors from protesting. It certainly is not unheard of that persons now seeking rezoning buy off neighborhood protestors. That, the market modelers say, should be encouraged in any event.[2] For those still quarrelsome, the existence of the anti-wipeout provision removes one of the most potent arguments—equity. No longer can they ask that embarrassing question, "Why should the developer be able

[2] B. Siegan, *Land Use Control Without Zoning* (1972); Ellickson, "Alternatives to Zoning: Covenants, Nuisance Rules, and Fines as Land Use Controls," 40 *University of Chicago Law Review* 681 (1973).

to profit from our loss?" They will still be heard, but perhaps not so well or so long.

PLAN BREAKING

Of course, under an anti-wipeout, windfall-recapture system, the multiple-family developer would not be as likely to ask for a rezoning anyway. Presently, if the planning or zoning for the area has any effect at all, it usually reduces prices in areas planned or zoned for unintensive uses. Therefore, a developer can make a profit if he options the unintensively planned and zoned land and secures its rezoning. He does not seek to develop where the planning and zoning indicate he should because land prices would be higher there and his profit would have to come from his building (sweat) efforts rather than from the rezoning. So it is that the present planning-zoning allocation of land-use system invites its own destruction. Development goes where the plan says it should not. The infrastructure improvements, implaced in accord with the plan, are inadequate because development is more intensive than planned in some areas; in other areas, broad avenues lead to modest development. Obviously, if the plan-breaker is taxed for his windfall, he would tend not to break the plan in the first instance.

SPRAWL

An anti-wipeout, windfall-recapture system may also tend to eliminate sprawl. The reason is as follows. While, as indicated earlier, some have suggested that regulation which eliminates all use should be considered valid, courts have seldom yet upheld such confiscation. Therefore, either some development must be allowed, e.g., on three or four minimum acre lots, or the property to be kept undeveloped must be purchased. There is generally a shortage of funds to purchase; and some worry about taking too much land out of the tax base; so instead it is regulated for unintensive development. Unintensive development is another name for sprawl.

Under an anti-wipeout, windfall-recapture scheme, windfall-recapture would produce funds to permit the purchase of lands not to be developed; alternatively, funds would be available so that compensatory regulations could be used. Compensatory regulation is a way to make severe regulation valid.

HORSETRADING

The present system has also resulted in an inefficient bargaining system over development permission exactions. The theory behind traditional American land-use controls is that they are general and are laid on a broad area after comprehensive study. Some windfalls and wipeouts may result, but at least, under such a theory, the original plan was done in the public interest. The governmental decision was not (in theory) focused on a particular parcel so as to cause a wipeout or windfall. Once zoned, the landowner had a reasonable expectation that he could develop as zoned. He did not have to get further permission.

The trouble with the theory is that it is a myth. There is really very little of the traditional American land-use control system left. Indeed, there is doubt that it ever existed. What is growingly evident is that no development of any significant type takes place by way of right. Discretion is exercised as to almost all development—subdivision permission, a rezoning, a zoning variance, a conditional use permit, or a building permit is used as a land-use control. And since discretion is involved, it can be conditioned. And it has been conditioned by exactions on development permissions. But this is a bargaining system of enormously inefficient dimensions. Compared with a systematic windfall-recapture device, it is as a cottage industry for manufacturing bicycles compares with General Motors.

This cottage system works like this. A city has an ordinance which is very vague as to what a developer must do to secure development permission. The developer then comes in with his drawings which indicate as little provision for public roads, parks, school sites, etc., as he thinks he can conceivably get away with. He does not usually find these minimums in the ordinance; rather he looks at what the city has required of the last developer. The city counters by demanding all sorts of things— fireplaces in the houses, shag roofs, larger public roads, bigger parks, etc. Gradually, and fraught with opportunities for abuse of discretion, equal protection and corruption, and at great cost of transactions to both the public and to the private developer, an agreement is reached. The public interest as represented in the bargain varies enormously from community to community; hardheaded businessmen running one city may be much less concerned about the livability of the new development than they are over how much of the public costs of new development can be laid on the developer to pass on to his customers.

The development permission exaction system is a windfall-recapture device, but it is a most inefficient one. Perhaps that is so in part because it is a reality without a theory. It just grew.

TWO WRONGS MAKE IT RIGHT

Finally, the absence of an anti-wipeout, windfall-recapture system has led to the failure to develop a more sensitive governmental response to government-induced harms and to what might be called "rapacious development."

Lack of Sensitivity—If one considered all of the private increases and decreases in value caused by all activities of government in gross, the winners would at least equal the losers. But if one examined the situations more carefully, one would see that some were terrible losers and others considerable winners. As a government becomes more civilized, terrible losers earn sympathy; and the government tries to do something about those situations. For example, over the years since the founding of our country, it is likely one could demonstrate that rules for compensation when property is taken by eminent domain have grown much more sensitive to individual situations. However, assuming that there are situations at any one time in which individuals are not being treated fairly, more sensitive treatment is delayed because one is faced with a kind of two-wrongs-make-it-right argument. The argument is that even though a particular wipeout situation is unjust, government should not pay for the wipeout since there was a chance of a windfall and government does not recapture windfalls. Therefore, I conclude, the goal of visiting less harm on individuals by their governments is linked with the need to recapture windfalls.

Rapacious Development—We are told that society must come to view land as a resource rather than as a commodity. I will not here examine that cliché in depth, for it might be found wanting. But when land is treated as a commodity, the image we are intended to have is that of the developer buying low, corrupting local government officials, building quickly, cheaply and badly, moving on, and leaving the community with a soon-to-develop slum. Meanwhile, he has made a large profit. However, this rapacious developer may defend his activities by pointing out that while the profit was great, the risk was also high. He can demonstrate that the development industry is a high-risk industry—many large and small developers go bankrupt yearly. Not infrequently today that is so because of what David Craig calls the iron whim of the public, namely, governments change their mind. Therefore, once the developer is in he strives to complete—rapaciously if necessary—and get out.

The point is, why should the development industry be such a high-risk industry? If land is a resource of fundamental importance, why do we not lower the risk as we do in the case of provision of electricity, or gas, or other public utility operations—or for that matter, lower the risk as we do in the case of banking or other quasi-public utilities where bankruptcies are so rare as to make national news when one occurs. Why should we allow a local community to throw a moratorium on a developer that causes bankruptcy or wastes resources simply because a moratorium may be constitutional? It may be constitutional; it may not be right. It may not lead that developer to socially conscious development the next time he tries to develop in some other community, that is, if he is still in business.

One concerned about rapacious development might pause to consider whether such development is partially only a self-help wipeout-avoidance technique induced by the developer's need to minimize arbitrary and capricious governmental decision-making. An anti-wipeout system is a risk-removal device. To the extent risks are removed, the rapacious developer no longer deserves so high a windfall. He need no longer be as rapacious about land development. He can "afford" to treat land as a resource, and thus it is preserved as a resource.

Techniques

Several mechanisms have been utilized or might be considered as windfall-recapture or anti-wipeout devices.

WINDFALL-RECAPTURE

Special Assessments—The special assessment is the first in time of the American devices. Whether it was so at all times or places, it was certainly true in some that developers merely drew lines on a map and sold off chunks of land. They did not consider it their responsibility to provide public facilities. At times, government used its general revenues to put in these facilities and thus make the lands utilizable. Perhaps the tradition of government so doing grew out of the pioneer spirit where one pioneer or settlement furnished the economic base for assisting the next.

But when government puts in the infrastructure and pays for it with general revenues, the newly-developed area enjoys enormous increases in value. With those public facilities in place, it increases in value considerably. So if the burden of putting those facilities in is on others, the owners of the developable area enjoy a windfall. Because there is a windfall, the notion that the infrastructure for new development should be at the expense of the existing community has been waning, and the special assessment was the first device generally applied to the task of imposing the infrastructure costs on the new development itself.

Under a special assessment, land (not building) is assessed up to its pro rata cost of the project, e.g., a street, and up to the amount of benefit received. Typically, the existing community picks up part of the cost; typically the amount of the assessment is nowhere near the amount of benefit received; typically special assessments are utilized for only local improvements.

The special assessment reached its peak use in the 1920s. In the great depression, landowners did not pay off the special assessments because much land became valueless. As a result, the bonds funded by assessments and sold to pay for the improvements became valueless. While local governments did not always stand behind this debt, their credit was nevertheless impaired.

During the depression, properties were even abandoned for property taxes, let alone for the typically higher special assessment burdens, and where communities had allowed subdivision without the provision of improvements, they inherited the worst possible tax-abandoned situations —subdivisions with a checkerboard of unimproved lots, some owned by a variety of people, some owned by the original developer and many "inherited" by the local government because of tax abandonment.

Ever since the bad experience with special assessments during the 1930s, they have not been the principal means used in America to impose the infrastructure costs on new development. But before considering the other devices, note an example of how special assessments might be used.

It is well known that when a fixed-rail mass transit system is built, land values increase dramatically around the stations. The owners of nearby land enjoy a windfall. There is little reason in theory, however, which would preclude use of a special assessment to recapture these increases in value. The funds raised could be used to help pay for the mass transit system or for other public purposes. Indeed, assuming that the plan of the community was to encourage intense development around mass transit stops, the high tax on land would help force intense development.

Subdivision Permission Exactions—With the demise of the special assessment as a windfall-recapture device, local governments turned to subdivision exactions as a means of loading the infrastructure cost of new development on the new development itself. In order to divide land and sell it nowadays, it is generally necessary to obtain subdivision permission from a local government. Before giving its final permission, the local government will require the developer to dedicate land for streets, parks, and perhaps school sites, improve the streets, and put in utilities such as sewer and water. Over the years local governments have imposed increasingly onerous exactions by way of dedication and improvement. Ferocious legal battles have been waged. Perhaps ninety percent of the case law and legal commentaries on subdivision deals with the exaction question. The war was won by local governments. While it is not yet everywhere clear, I think that ultimately a developer can legally be required to put in all public improvements required by the subdivision, the only limit perhaps being that the requirements laid on the new development cannot be greater than the benefits the new development receives from the improvements. Note the similarity to the limitation on special assessments.

The main advantage of the subdivision exaction scheme is that it assures the building of public improvements before the subdivided land is sold, rather than afterward. A major disadvantage is the bargaining that takes place and the shopping around by developers who try to find communities which are still willing to subsidize new development from the wealth of the existing community.

Subdivision Fees—Just as special assessments begat subdivision dedication and improvement requirements, these requirements begat a variant subdivision exaction—fees in lieu of dedication and improvement. For example, rather than requiring a subdivider to dedicate a park out of his land, he might be required to pay a fee in lieu thereof, which fee the local government would use with others to provide a park in some other location. Great legal battles were fought over this concept as well, for the direct relationship between the improvement and the subdivision was lost. But we are now at the point where it should be clear that if the park benefits the subdivision burdened by the fee, it need not be located within the subdivision—we are almost at the point where the fee is proper as a realization that the new development should pay something to buy into the existing community infrastructure.

Development Permission Exactions—It should be noted, at this point, that while the exaction system began with subdivision, it has now spread to all development permissions—rezonings, zoning variances, special use permits and even building permits. While still loosely associated with the need for infrastructure that the new development will generate, the relationship is tenuous. Particularly if it is a fee, the exaction begins to look very much like a charge for development permission. When applied to a rezoning, for example, it looks like an upzoning tax—a windfall-recapture device which has been suggested by people such as Marion Clawson.

Development Taxes—The genealogy is complete when one considers another device that grew out of subdivision fees. Developer resistance to ever-increasing subdivision exactions led to enactment of state laws constraining the use of exactions. Cities were thwarted in their ever-growing tendency to impose all the governmental costs of new development on the development itself.

Therefore local governments tried an end run. It was successful in California where cities have general power to impose business license taxes to raise revenue. A liquor license, for example, is an expensive license in many communities because it is used as a revenue raiser. So cities in California began imposing business license taxes on developers measured by, e.g., how many bedrooms were constructed by the developer. Thus, if a developer built a project with 1,000 units having 3,000 bedrooms and the tax was $1,000 per bedroom, the developer's tax would yield $3,000,000. That will buy a lot of street, park, sewer, water, school, etc., improvements. Indeed, since a business license tax goes into the general fund, there is no requirement that it be spent for those purposes. It could be used to pay salaries of policemen. A California court upheld the tax idea in 1971 and it has swept the state, many cities adopting the idea. Subdivision exactions could become a passé subject as the new license fee on developers, or developers' tax or impact tax come to be accepted. And it was rejected by courts in Arizona and Florida; meanwhile, the Nevada legislature authorized it—in lieu of using subdivision exactions.

Capital Gains Tax—Though it did not evolve out of the continuum I have been describing, the capital gains tax is a windfall-recapture device of sorts. The opportunity to deduct capital losses is an anti-wipeout device. But the capital gains tax is not justified on the grounds that government should recapture some of the gains caused by it or others in the community. It is justified because realized gain is income, and there are federal and state income taxes in this country. To say the capital gains tax is a windfall-recapture device is to say that an income tax is a windfall-recapture device, which it is only in a very broad sense. But the capital gains tax does not distinguish between real and personal property and, thus far, this paper is addressed only to windfalls and wipeouts to *land*owners. Moreover, few if any local governments have capital gains taxes; yet it is their public works projects or their regulations which cause many of the windfalls and wipeouts.

Still, capital gains taxes might be affirmatively considered as a windfall-recapture device. It has often been argued that capital gains should be taxed at ordinary income rates. The argument can be made specially vigorously as to land, which often gains in value directly by governmental activity. The state of Vermont, concerned with rapid turnover of land by out-of-state speculators, investors, and developers, enacted a special additional capital gains tax on land sales only in 1972. New Zealand enacted such a law in 1973 and the English Conservative government, sensitive about their long failure to recapture "betterment," proposed to do so in late 1973 with a stiff capital gains tax on land.

Transfer Taxes—Remember the documentary stamp tax the federal government used to impose of $.55 per $500 of the sales price of real estate. States and localities have taken over that tax, now abandoned by the federal government. The tax might be used more broadly so that a tax bite of more substantial amounts is levied every time property changes hands. Of course, in its traditional form it is not a windfall-recapture device. For example, property may sell for less than it was bought for, but the tax would still be due. Nevertheless, one could imagine a transfer tax which would apply only if there were a gain and would be measured by the gain. So defined, it begins to look much like a capital gains tax.

Unearned Increment Tax—An unearned increment tax is another leading device for windfall-recapture, but it has never been tried in the United States, so far as I have been able to discern. It bears similarities to the special assessment and to the capital gains tax. The notion is that land increases in value due to public activity and private activity of others. As a result, there is an *unearned* increment which might be recaptured on such taxable events as sale or transfer or—to distinguish it from the capital gains tax—at the time development permission is obtained, or at the time the permission is utilized, or even after a period of years if no other taxable event occurs. It also differs from the capital gains tax in that a concept of capital loss may not be included—it is a one-way street—there is no compensation for unearned decrement. It is also limited to land, which distinguishes it from the capital gains tax. It may have a provision for adjusting for inflation, that is, the increment may be measured only in terms of real increase. It differs from a special assessment in that there is no need to form a special assessment district and make an assessment for each benefit-producing improvement. And benefit is not measured in anticipation, as in the case of the special assessment, but at a taxable event. Moreover, it could be used to recapture benefits flowing from other than public improvements. Public regulatory activities, e.g., rezonings, or other private activity in the vicinity, could cause a recapturable increment.

The unearned increment tax gets good marks from many economists, though it comes in many varieties and is difficult either to endorse or condemn. The English tried it in the Land Commission Act of 1967. Called the betterment levy, it was repealed by the Conservative government when it came to power in 1970, though its merits were probably greater than the previous English experiment with recapturing land-value increments, which will be described later. The State of New South Wales, Australia, enacted a Land Development Contribution Law in 1970, an unearned increment tax, but both political parties came to agree in 1973 that it should be repealed. It is therefore surprising to see that New Zealand passed the Property Speculation Tax in 1973, which has some attributes of an unearned increment tax—the mere title of the Act suggests as much—though it also looks somewhat like a special capital gains tax on land.

Single Tax—The single tax is the last windfall-recapture device one might consider. Popularized by Henry George, it attracts converts as each new generation of students of tax policy considers the relation of taxation and land. It has never gone anywhere in this country and is not likely to go anywhere in the future. The notion of the single tax is that the only tax should be an annual property tax on land, excluding buildings. Those parcels of land which became more valuable because of public activity or other private activity would, of course, be assessed at a very high level reflecting their market value as contrasted with property which was not very valuable because of the absence of public and private value-causing activities in the environs.

As an annual tax, it differs from the others and might not be considered a windfall-recapture device. For example, assume that the property tax (now on land and buildings) is converted to a land value only tax. Effective property tax rates these days are about two percent, that is, the typical real property owner pays $2.00 every year for every $100 of market value of his property. Assume further that about half of the value of all property now in the property tax base is in improvements, which means that the property tax on land only would have to be levied at a $4.00 rate to raise the same amount of revenue as is now raised on both land and improvements. Suppose finally that a transit station is built in a neighborhood and that a parcel of property thereby increases in value from $10,000 to $110,000. The increment would be $100,000, but the *annual* tax would increase only from $400 to $4,400, only 4.4 percent of the total increase.

While one can make the illustration more sophisticated by considering capitalization of the tax in land value and discounting and the like, the point is a simple one, the land value tax does not recapture the increment at one time, as the others do. On the other hand, note that a special assessment does not typically do so either. While the assessment debt is created in one year, it is usually payable over a period of years. The difference is that the special assessment is fixed at one time, the land value tax varies as market value varies.

The main contribution of Henry George and the land value tax school of thought is the notion that private landowners have no right to the increase in value created by others, be the others private or public. That philosophical note underlies all of the windfall-recapture schemes.

WIPEOUT AVOIDANCE

Damage from Public Improvements—The story on wipeout avoidance is shorter. There are few techniques used in America, except in limited situations. Consider public improvements first. If a governmental entity acquires a site, of course, the landowner gets paid. That he should is not debatable. The federal and all state constitutions require it. We do not expect the landowner to absorb such wipeouts. Similarly, if only part of a site is acquired, the landowner not only receives compensation for the site, but usually receives damages to the remainder of his property caused by the acquisition. Thus, if half of one's property is acquired for a sewage treatment plant, the landowner gets paid for the property acquired and damages due to the fact that the remainder of his property is likely to be less valuable because of the sewage treatment plant acquisition.

Generally speaking, however, the landowner whose property adjoins the sewer plant, no part of whose property is taken, but who may find his property value substantially affected, is wiped out. The government hardly ever pays in those situations. Of course, sometimes neighboring property is benefited as the result of acquisition. These windfalls are not recaptured under American practice.

The English call the externalities that flow from public acquisition "injurious affection," and in the Land Compensation Act of 1973, lands adversely affected by public improvements, no part of which are taken, are entitled to compensation in some circumstances. It might be considered in America.

Damages in Nuisance—Nuisance law is a wipeout avoidance technique. Theoretically, if a neighbor uses land in a way which produces externalities, those landowners burdened by the externalities may be able to sue in nuisance. An injunction might be obtained against the use, but that is a rather drastic remedy, so damages are often allowed instead. In effect, the court permits the nuisance to continue but allows those landowners burdened by it to be paid by the nuisance-creator.

Nuisance law has not evolved significantly. One of the reasons is that governmental entities have been given a virtual monopoly over control of land use externalities through land use controls such as zoning. The assumption is that if a local government permits a particular use, the action can hardly constitute a nuisance. Similarly, courts are very loath to declare a governmental use of land a nuisance, though there has been some evolution of that legal relief as the courts become sensitized to the fact that governmental entities are the worst violators of the environment.

Compensable Regulations—More is being heard these days about compensable regulations. I explain. One of the reasons few wipeout avoidance techniques have developed in America is that regulation of land has seldom been so severe as to cause a total or near total wipeout. Rather than sustain the regulation and require some compensation to be paid, courts have invalidated severe regulations. That is anti-wipeout protection by denying government its will, a topic not here relevant, since I am concerned with adjustments that permit government to act, not rules that prevent governmental action.

With the new environmentalism, however, regulations are now much tougher. Some courts have been willing to go along with the tougher regulations and, as a result, landowners have legislators discussing compensable regulations. Many other courts which would not sustain tough regulations would do so if some compensation were paid to the regulated landowner. The American Law Institute is developing a Model Land Development Code which contains compensable regulation provisions.

Since noncompensatory regulations severely limiting use often turn out to be transitory, compensable regulations should involve a windfall-recapture provision. When the regulators change their mind and permit land to develop, the owners may gain a windfall. If the landowner has been compensated for the regulation, it would obviously be equitable to recapture the windfall when the regulation changes to permit development.

WINDFALLS FOR WIPEOUTS

The most exciting techniques are those that simultaneously deal with the windfall and wipeout problems.

Zoning by Eminent Domain—Zoning by eminent domain is one such technique.[3] The idea is over a half century old and stems from the early days of zoning, when it was unclear whether the courts would hold zoning by regulation valid. It was actually used in St. Paul and Minneapolis and Kansas City, where areas zoned by eminent domain still exist today. Interestingly, the technique also involves special assessments.

It works as follows. Assume there is an unzoned area or city. The city decides that certain areas should be used for commerce, other areas for residence, and yet others for industrial purposes. That constitutes the zoning feature. The eminent domain feature is that the city then acquires the development rights for all other purposes than those permitted under the zoning for the area. Landowners are paid damages to the extent that taking the development rights lowers values, thus wipeout is avoided. But, in that hypothetical city, since the zoning has just shifted values around, as is always the case with zoning, some property is worth more than it was before. The property worth more has received a benefit which is specially assessed—windfalls are thus recaptured and used to pay off damages. In short, windfalls for wipeouts.

Every time any zoning is changed, the benefit and the damage are measured and the transfer payments, if any, are made. Routinized and computerized, the system might be reasonably simple to administer. As actually applied in Minnesota and Missouri, the concept proved inflexible, but there is nothing inherent in the idea which requires such a result.

Development Rights Transfer—The windfalls for wipeouts technique presently getting the most attention is called development rights transfer.[4] Consider an example of how it might work. A 2-story historic building is located in a central business district which is zoned for 50-story buildings. Noting a market for a new skyscraper, the owner of the historic building decides to tear it down and construct the large building. The city's historical society seeks foundation funds to acquire the historic site. That effort fails, and the city is asked to pass a zoning regulation requiring that the private landowner maintain the historic building. The city decides the proposed regulation would be unconstitutional, and the historic building is ultimately lost.

Under developmental rights transfer, however, the city could order the landlord to maintain the historic building, but, as compensation, would permit the landowner to sell his 48 stories of unused development rights to a neighbor, who can then build a 98-story building. These objectives are thereby accomplished:

[3] The fullest recent discussion of the idea I know of is Hagman, "Implementation of Land Use Planning in the Political Process," in *Land Use Planning* 128, 133 (T. Box ed. 1972).

[4] The fullest exploration is Costonis, "Development Rights Transfer: An Exploratory Essay," 83 *Yale Law Journal* 75 (1973).

—The landowner avoids a wipeout.
—The historic building is preserved.
—The overall permitted density of downtown goes unchanged.

The technique can be applied to other situations, e.g., marshland can be zoned so as to prevent all use, but the owners would be given development rights which could be used elsewhere or sold to others who can then develop to higher than normal intensities elsewhere.

Public Ownership—Finally, these are windfall-recapture and wipeout-avoidance devices that involve public ownership of land or development rights therein. Obviously, if the government owns the land, there are no private windfalls or wipeouts from land ownership. But public ownership is outside the scope of matters considered in this paper.

Windfalls for Wipeouts: Can It—Should It Be Done?

Can and should we develop an anti-wipeout or a windfall-recapture, or both systems in America? As previously indicated, unless both are adopted, I regard it as rather unlikely and probably undesirable for either to be adopted. Whether both should be adopted needs further consideration.

OTHER BENEFITS

While the anti-wipeout, windfall-recapture techniques previously described are included because they address both the windfall and wipeout issue, and thus result in equity, or better land-use control, or both, only a few of the techniques discussed were invented for those purposes. They were variously promoted to preserve open space, to remove slums, to raise revenues, to preserve historic sites, to reduce land prices, or to inhibit speculation. Those are all worthy goals, and any proposed system should also seek to address them so as to gain the support of the constituency for those goals.

ADVERSE SIDE EFFECTS

Like any medicine, adoption of the anti-wipeout, windfall-recapture system can have side effects. By tracing the results of some of the actual experiments it is possible to anticipate some of the adverse side effects and devise a formula which reduces them. One difficulty is that almost all of the experience is foreign. And, while this foreign experience is represented in Australia, Canada, England, and New Zealand, which countries have customs, laws, and values much like those in America, the lessons learned in those countries cannot with complete assurance be replicated in America. It is also possible to build theoretic models and thus anticipate consequences, but I have considerable skepticism that a model will identify all the side effects. That leaves one with some experiments. These involve risk, but an advantage of the federal system is that there are numerous labs for experimentation. Moreover, experiments in anti-wipeout or windfall-recapture or both will be undertaken in any event and hopefully the initial experiments will be well considered. One bad experiment may be enough to end an otherwise good idea.

WHAT IS A WINDFALL?

Deciding what increases in value are to be recaptured is a basic difficulty. Few would suggest that values caused by "sweat" efforts should be recaptured. For example, if a farmer's property increased in value by ten percent because he spent that amount of money improving its drainage, to recapture that increase would discourage him from making the improvement. Only zealous environmental status quoism interested in disincentives to any development would urge recapture of that kind of increase.

More persons could be persuaded that increases in value caused by others, whether the others be governmental or private actors, should be recaptured on the theory that the increase is unearned. Perhaps even a majority would agree that when government acts for the common weal, as of course is the only way it can act, it is fair to recapture windfall caused by those activities.

It may be difficult to define what is to be recaptured. For example, how to distinguish between earned and unearned increment? Suppose a developer options land at $10,000,000 and secures final development permission making the property worth $50,000,000. A $40,000,000 "profit" looks obscenely unearned. But suppose the developer spent $30,000,000 jumping all the tough environmental hurdles with increasing amounts at risk. A $10,000,000 profit on a $40,000,000 investment may well be a justifiable entrepreneurial reward.

WHAT IS A WIPEOUT?

If majority support cannot be obtained for windfall recapture, more could be expected to support it if the system also involved anti-wipeout protection. Few could be added as supporters if anti-wipeout protection were extended only to those who waste land by neglect and negligence, thereby leading to its devaluation. More would give protection from other private action, e.g., there are those who would agree that the law of private nuisance should be expanded. And the current American interest in compensable regulations and the English extension of "injurious affection" concepts to lands no part of which has been taken suggests considerable support for the notion that wipeouts caused by governmental activity should be redressed.

WHAT GOVERNMENT?

In the past, windfalls and wipeouts have been caused by all levels of government if one considers all governmental acquisition and development activities. But until recently only local general purpose governments have had any significant land-use controls. Windfalls and wipeouts caused by controls were caused by them, not by regional, state, federal, or special district government regulation. They were also the general plan-making governments, so to the extent that an anti-wipeout, windfall-recapture system is motivated by a desire to improve the planning system, one might consider applying the windfalls for wipeouts system only to local general purpose governments.

The picture is no longer so clear. State and regional control is *the* hot news story of the 70s and the federal presence is substantial. There may be one difference between local and regional, state or federal control, which difference might lead to a conclusion that a windfalls for wipeouts system should be limited to local controls. Local controls are often imposed on a specific parcel of property, so that the owner's windfall or wipeout is directly caused by governmental action, and the government would have to be blind not to know that. Regional, state, and federal controls are not as often so focused, though under the federal air and water acts, even the federal government will be giving permits for particular projects. Regional, state, or federal control might be more objective because the regulators and regulatees are not as likely to belong to the same social set. On the other hand, maybe they will, because the movement to pass land-use control decision-making upward is paralleled by the demise of the small developer. Large government and large developers do operate at the same level. Further, special governments such as water and sewer districts turn out these days to be de facto growth control agencies. As such districts do or do not provide water or sewer services, they, not the general purpose local government, unleash the windfall or wipeout, regardless of how the general purpose government plans or regulates. Perhaps, it will be difficult to draw any lines distinguishing among types of government when designing the windfalls for wipeouts system. The line may have to be drawn arbitrarily and justified on the ground that at least the law is moving in the right direction, but it is not tidy to have a landowner's rights depend on what type of government is acting.

WHAT TYPE OF ACTIVITY?

Windfalls and wipeouts usually occur as a result of governmental acquisition and building activities or because of land-use control regulations. But what are land-use regulations? And how direct must the acquisition and building effect be? There are two classic illustrations of the difficulty. Suppose that a strip commercial area is fronted by a street on which parking is permitted. Subsequently, parking is precluded. The merchants are wiped out. Is the traffic regulation a land-use control? One is not likely to find it discussed in books on land-use controls. The other classic involves this supposition: A new interstate highway is built and, under windfalls for wipeouts, adjustments are made for landowners gaining or losing along it. But what of the owners of the service stations, the motels, and the advertising signs along the old highway, now a local street two miles away? They have been wiped out as effectively as if they were zoned out of existence.

Line-drawing is acceptable if it is rational and if the place where the line is drawn is fairly clear to all. The latter reason, for example, is probably why landowners are paid for damages when some land is taken in eminent domain and they are not paid when no land is taken. It is a sharp, clear line. There may be enough common agreement as to what are and are not land-use controls so as to draw a fairly sharp line from other governmental *regulatory* activity, other governmental activity, or private activity which impacts values on private lands. Whether it is rational to draw the line at any of those places is less certain.

WHO IS A WIPEOUTEE/WINDFALLEE?

Generally, we think of landowners as the ones we want to protect from wipeouts. That we should is curious in the view of some. For example, the authors of *The Taking Issue*[5] subtitle one of their points, "Land Use Regulations Deserve Equal Status with Other Regulations," and argue that severe land-use regulations should not be invalidated any more than would regulations on other types of property. For those who believe that severe regulations of land should not be sustained, it is necessary to venture some distinctions. I have suggested in the Harvard Law Review that:

. . . land use controls seldom deal with basic, important issues of health and safety, as other regulations might; regulations of other property ordinarily do not have drastic and direct effects on values; and such regulations do not have as precise locational effects as do land use controls, which may force particular property owners to serve the public interest without public expense.

Frankly, it is hard to know whether the distinctions do add up to a difference.

A skeptic of windfalls for wipeouts would argue that one who loses on the stock market as a result of governmental activity is not compensated, so why compensate landowners? There is one distinction that landowners sometimes make. Real property owners pay property taxes; personal property owners seldom do. Therefore, landowners can argue with some justification that they have been paying taxes over the years, often on

[5] *Supra* note 1.

undeveloped property which is (presumably) valued for tax purposes at its market value, the market anticipating a much more intensive use than it is zoned for, or at least anticipating the use for which it is zoned. When the zoning is rolled back, landowners argue they have been treated unfairly. They have been paying taxes for years in expectation of development, have not received services commensurate with the tax, yet they are denied their expectation. The answer to this plea for fairness might well be that the property tax is a tax on wealth in a sense—when one has wealth, he is taxed for that wealth; if it has now been taken away, one will not be taxed for that which he no longer possesses.

The most fundamental classification in property law is between real and personal property. Why real property is treated differently than personal property is a subject of a jurisprudential, treatise-length discussion. They are different, so that landowner windfallees-wipeoutees should be treated differently than stockowner windfallees-wipeoutees may be a matter of unexplainable faith. Note, the same faith may perhaps explain why windfall-recapture proposals are limited to real property.

But the question of who is a landowner remains. Consider some examples. In December 1973, the Regents of the University of California sued the U. S. Environmental Protection Agency because a $450 per year per parking place tax was to be levied on the parking lots under the Clean Air Act. A similar burden was levied throughout much of the nation on parking lots in regions where air was poor. The intended effect was that students would no longer drive their cars to school. Why did the University sue? It had built a number of parking structures and had issued bonds to pay them off.

Suppose first the bondholders were limited to revenues from the parking structures. The University was not then wiped out. Suppose that the University had to pay off the bonds regardless of the adequacy of the revenues? The University then suffered a wipeout. If the University suffered no wipeout, the bondholders would. Students whose automobiles were worth less may suffer a wipeout. Perhaps the University would not suffer a wipeout even if it had to pay off the bonds. The same Clean Air Act probably resulted in student demand for housing near the University—the parking structures might well have value as a place to park mobile homes for students.

Consider one more example. A landowner options land to a developer who secures a rezoning, gets financing, and starts to build. Only one store gets built and leased before the property is visited by a moratorium. A moratorium causes a wipeout, but to whom? Typically the former landowner, the developer, the lending institution, and the lessee will all have some interest in the land. Deciding who should be compensated is difficult. Fortunately, there is experience with the matter, because similar problems arise when land is acquired by eminent domain.

In the case of regulation, there may be some question whether payment is due at all when risk is spread widely. Recall an observation made earlier. Land development now increasingly tends to be undertaken by multinational conglomerates. A particular project or a particular asset owned by them might be wiped out by governmental action, but the corporation is not going to be so wiped out. The loss is distributed perhaps among millions of stockholders and possibly in several countries. If the risk is thus distributed, why should government have an anti-wipeout system to distribute risk? That may be a very good question. Equity may suggest limitation of anti-wipeout protection to owners with low risk distribution capability. Of course, windfall-recapture and wipeout-avoidance systems are also justified as a means of improving land-use controls; equity requirements are not the only motivation.

CAN WINDFALLS AND WIPEOUTS BE MEASURED?

Measuring increases and decreases in the value of real property is a difficult task. Appraising is an art; the appraiser usually need only decide total value. He need not decide, for example, what value was caused by "sweat" efforts, what value by the private action of others, what value by governmental activity, and what value by particular kinds of governments or particular kinds of governmental activity. Depending on what part of an increase is to be recaptured and what part of a decrease is to be compensated, the appraiser may have to make such fine distinctions.

The valuation problem may be so great that the available means of measuring will define the windfall to be collected or the wipeout to be reimbursed—for example, a special capital gains tax on the sale of land might be adopted because we are familiar with how to measure gain or loss. If the tax worked like a normal capital gains tax, however, the difference between the purchase and the sale price minus the "sweat" efforts would be the windfall to be recaptured or the wipeout to be reimbursed.

But I am hopeful that measuring the windfall or wipeout will not be so difficult that it dictates the decision on what part of the increase or decrease will be considered the windfall or wipeout. The property tax assessment system may be the most attractive alternative on which to build a windfall and wipeout measuring scheme.

That one should suggest such a historically lawless, arbitrary system as the basis for any further system of value measurement deserves some explanation. A review of developments among the states would show that at least some are within striking distance of annual, computer-aided, pseudoscientific, professional property tax assessment. Indeed, my hidden agenda in windfalls for wipeouts includes a strong hope that it will stimulate realization of such a property tax assessment system. Better assessment is substantially a matter of devoting more resources to the task. The added resources can be justified by the need to have the property tax assessment system provide the measurement function for the windfall-recapture, anti-wipeout system as well. Other benefits would result—gains and losses in real property could be used in evidence in eminent domain proceedings; the real estate industry would have a better source of information; and society would have a better device for measuring economic effects that translate into land values.

While I do not know whether building the measuring system on property tax assessments is precedented, I am not dissuaded by the lack of precedent. The countries most like America (Australia, Canada, England, New Zealand) whose windfall-recapture, wipeout-avoidance schemes were not based on property tax assessments, do not have American property tax assessment systems. In most of those countries either an annual (rent), not a capital (market value) system is used, or different bases are used, e.g., in Australia and New Zealand some jurisdictions use an annual, some a capital (land and buildings), and some a land value only system, and the effective burden of the property tax is much lower, so it is not worth the effort to have more than rough assessments.

In the United States, however, the property tax is generally a significant tax, and is everywhere based on market values of land and buildings. While assessors are now only concerned with market values each year, the data are available to measure *changes* in value of each property. Whether assessment systems can be further developed to separate out and measure changes caused by only certain types of activities is a matter for further inquiry.

ADMINISTRATION

The American system of land-use controls is more pervasive and complex than is necessary. An anti-wipeout, windfall-recapture system will take administration, will involve some start-up costs, and does add some complexity. But since I shrink from making recommendations that make public land-use controls more pervasive, complex, and difficult to administer, it is my fond hope that any anti-wipeout, windfall-recapture system adopted will not add any net increase of complexity and administration. Indeed, a goal of the windfall-recapture and anti-wipeout system is to reduce control by lowering the amount of public decision-making energy that is devoted to resolving who-gets-the-goodies squabbles. The market, aided by the windfall for wipeout system, can accommodate much of that squabble. Therefore, it is hoped, the present system plus the windfalls for wipeout system will result in a net *decrease* in complexity and administration. Yet, it is further hoped, public decision-making will be better because it can be focused on the truly public dimensions, not the private detail.

The windfalls for wipeouts concept is one America should consider. But is the concept in some version one America should adopt?

Lyle C. Fitch and Ruth P. Mack

6

Land Banking

This chapter is mainly concerned with the possibilities of improving the process of urban physical development by the government's acquiring title, or development rights, to undeveloped land well in advance of its conversion to its intended purpose. Two main types of program are considered:

1. The acquisition, well in advance of actual need, of land for specific public purposes (schools, sewage disposal plants, roadways, parks and open space); and
2. Acquisition of large tracts of land for the purpose of enabling "better" (however defined) urban development on a medium or large scale.

These two aspects of "land banking" serve rather different purposes.

Acquisition for Specific Purposes

In summary, the objectives of the first type of program—advance acquisition of specific limited sites—are to (1) enhance productivity of public operations by siting physical facilities in optimal locations; (2) decrease costs of land acquisition; and (3) preserve options respecting possible fu-

LYLE C. FITCH *is president of the Institute of Public Administration, New York. In 1957–61 he was successively first deputy and city administrator of the City of New York. Dr. Fitch has served as consultant on urban transportation planning to federal, state, and city government agencies and has written several books and many articles on urban planning, finance, administration, and transportation.* RUTH P. MACK *is director of Economic Studies of the Institute of Public Administration. Formerly a member of the senior research staff of the National Bureau of Economic Research, Dr. Mack has also been a professor of City University of New York and Yale. An advisor to state and federal agencies, she has written several books and papers on problems of planning.*

ture decisions. Or, to state the obverse, the purpose is to avoid the consequences of not having taken thought for the future, and of having to accept poorly located sites, paying exhorbitant prices for acquiring and clearing land, and having to forego altogether land for certain purposes such as parks, playgrounds, and preservation of open space for environmental or aesthetic reasons.

These are for the most part well-recognized *public* purposes.[1] The thing which inhibits the acquisition, in advance of need, of land for such facilities has to do less with the public character of the intended use (except in a few instances) than with the uncertainty of future needs. It is also difficult to finance advance acquisitions of land, particularly in the face of uncertainty. But that uncertainty can be dealt with. When land values are rising, as is general in developing urban areas, a municipality which has overestimated its land requirements may suffer no worse fate than having to sell its excess land at a profit. The nature of the benefit and cost calculation will be discussed in a later section.

The method of financing even for such limited purposes, however, presents a more serious problem in many communities, which must go into debt and thereby raise taxes for debt service while at the same time taking land off the tax rolls. Even if a policy of advance acquisition pays off in the long run, city officials and councils are typically elected for two to four years and are likely to take the attitude that "in the long run we'll all be dead anyway, but in the short run we'll be dead politically if we raise taxes." Possible escape hatches from this dilemma are later discussed.

Acquisition for General Urban Development

Large tracts are usually acquired primarily for planning and building large communities—new towns or planned unit developments (PUD's). On regional scale, large acquisitions may be required for such objectives as the preservation of open space, including forests and wetlands, for recreation, environmental and climatic control and other ecological purposes. Here, however, we are concerned primarily with improving urban development.

The presumptive superiority of planned urban development is predicated upon the notion that typical American-style development, with myriad residential, shopping-center, and other developers each doing "their thing" under the widely variegated controls of the numerous local jurisdictions of most metropolitan areas, is inefficient, unaesthetic, and often described in pejorative terms: spread city, urban sprawl, or the

---

1 Each of these objections and ways in which they can be pursued is discussed in *Advance Land Acquisition by Local Governments, Benefit Cost Analysis as an Aid to Policy* by Donald C. Shoup and Ruth P. Mack, Institute of Public Administration for the United States Department of Housing and Urban Development, Washington, D.C., 1966.

slurb. Such development, it is thought, maximizes travel. It does not efficiently locate centers for employment, for residence, and for other activities in relation to each other in ways that economize on transportation requirements. Moreover, it requires a system of random access to activity centers which can be provided only by the motor vehicle, thus putting an extra burden on the atmosphere, on urban space, and on the many persons who cannot drive or have no automobile. Private small-scale developers have no immediate incentive to provide either recreational facilities or open spaces, and no reason to protect the environment.

Another deficiency is that developers, not having the right of eminent domain, pick up land where they can find it. This creates leapfrog patterns which increase the cost of utilities and transportation.

Communities which develop in such a hit-and-miss fashion frequently lack vital relationships to each other and to their central cities. A familiar manifestation on the American scene has been the wide separation of workshops and bedrooms and the homogenization of suburbs, along with segregation of racial and income groups. Few would maintain that these deficiencies of urban development can be overcome completely by any practicable amount of planning. But theory and precedent here and abroad both argue that it should be possible to produce something better than the urban sprawl, strip development, inefficient and dangerous transportation, and destruction of environment which characterize much recent American urban development.

James Rouse, developer of the new town of Columbia, testified before the House Committee on Banking and Currency in 1966:

> The most advanced planning and zoning concepts of America today are inadequate to preserve our forests and stream valleys and maintain open spaces. They cannot produce well-formed communities with a rich variety of institutions and activities and a wide range of choice in housing density, type, price, and rent. As a matter of fact, zoning has become almost the guarantee of sprawl rather than protection against it.[2]

(Columbia, it should be noted, involved the assembly by secret agents in the dead of night of some 20 square miles of land.)

Government Capacities for Land Assembly

In principle, government has the capacity for large-scale land assembly for planned community building which only exceptional private developers can muster.

First, it has a greater capacity for assembling large tracts through the

[2] Hearings before the Committee on Banking and Currency, 89 Cong., 2nd sess. (1966); *Demonstration Cities, Housing, and Urban Development, and Urban Mass Transit,* Part II, p. 1048.

use of a combination of negotiation and the power of eminent domain. As previously noted, where there are many parcels to be acquired, the job of assembling large tracts is usually beyond private developers. For instance, the overall success of land acquisition for Columbia has somewhat overshadowed the fact that there were many holdouts whose land could not be acquired. These remain as intrusive enclaves in the planned community, whose ownership pattern, it has been said, "resembles a Swiss cheese." The problem could have been handled by the power of eminent domain.

Second is the capacity to assume large front-end costs and to wait long periods for the return—a capacity which, we have seen, few private developers or financing agencies possess. The more foresighted the program the lengthier the waiting period is likely to be—Stockholm held land for up to 30 years prior to development.

Third, a government of appropriate jurisdictional scale can reduce, by good planning and judicious use of land-use controls, other risks associated with large development projects. Such risks are so formidable as to convince some writers that new-town development is a losing game for private developers.

Land Banking Abroad

Public acquisition of land as an instrument for guiding urban development is nothing new. It has been used extensively abroad. Stockholm comes first to mind. An implacably conservative government around the turn of the century acquired all the farmlands surrounding the then-existing city. The measure appealed to the business-minded burghers of the day as an exercise in prudent foresight for the future by avoiding both inappropriate development of the capital city and preserving for the public purse increases in land value accruing with urban development.

Such foresight enabled the Stockholm authorities after World War II to debate various options respecting the configuration of urban expansion. The benefits of such debates have been demonstrated in the city's famed suburban communities of Vallingby, Farsta, and others. These are attractively planned, separated by green space from the core city and each other, and efficiently linked by public transportation and highways. The planning concepts were not simply the natural result of the city owning the land on which new communities could be built—there was vigorous conflict over whether city growth should follow more conventional patterns—but the style, techniques and management of growth actually employed would not have been possible in the absence of municipal land ownership. Meanwhile, the land acquisition program has continued; about half of Stockholm's recent development has been on land acquired since World War II.

Other large-scale programs have been implemented in Germany, Israel,

Hong Kong, Canberra (Australia), Denmark, and Norway (Oslo is said to have the largest reservoir of undeveloped land of any European city). The English new towns have been built on land acquired for the purpose by development corporations which incorporate in one entity the several processes required to build a new town—planning, development control, land acquisition, and actual construction.[3]

North American Experience

Foreign experience, though extensive and varied, may be limited in its applicability to the American scene. But there has been notable use of public land acquisition for urban development in the provinces of Alberta and Saskatchewan, Canada, which may have something in common with the U. S., particularly in the conflicts over local and provincial government roles in the development process (as in Alberta). Another important precedent has been set in the Commonwealth of Puerto Rico, which has legislation enabling the public acquisition of large tracts, involving the following steps:

> The Land Administration prepares an "Ambito," identifying land designated for acquisition and indicating the quantities of land that may be required for future use. After the Ambito has been approved by the Puerto Rican Planning Board notice is published. The purchase price of the land at whatever times the acquisitions are actually made, will be the market value prevailing *at the time of the notice.* The procedure has been upheld by the courts, as a proper exercise of the government's land acquisition and eminent domain powers for the social welfare.[4]

On the mainland, federal land ownership originally was widespread, most of the country having been at one time in a public land bank. John W. Reps recalls that L'Enfant's plan for Washington, D. C., which ranks as "one of the most outstanding urban planning accomplishments in history," was made possible by public ownership of the entire site. A number of colonial cities and territorial capitals were planned and built on public land. "The publicly planned community usually had wider streets, more generous allocation of open space, more numerous sites for public and semi-public buildings, and greater emphasis on building beauty." [5] Much of Manhattan Island was at one time in public ownership, and New

[3] For a fine discussion of the characteristics of these and North American experience in land banking, see *Public Land Acquisition for New Communities and the Control of Urban Growth: Alternative Strategies* by Kermit C. Parsons, Harriet L. Budke, Simone Clemhout, Paul B. Farrell, James L. Prost, Ernest F. Roberts (Ithaca: Center for Urban Development Research, Cornell University. March 1973) pp. 1–26.

[4] *Ibid.*, pp. 13 and 14. Puerto Rico vs. Rosso, 1967.

[5] John W. Reps, "Public Land and Urban Development Policy," in Marian Clawson, *Modernizing Urban Land Policy,* Johns Hopkins University Press, 1973.

York derived much of its early revenues from leases, dock rents, and other miscellaneous fees, rather than from the sale of property. In 1844, the council authorized the sale of public real estate to reduce city indebtedness. Most of the Central Park site was sold off in early years and later had to be repurchased for some $5.4 million. As Reps points out, the city

> neither received the maximum possible income from its real estate nor did it use its vast holdings of land at the urban fringe to carry out a plan having any special merit. By contrast, the city of Savannah, Georgia, used its ownership of land at the urban fringe to achieve planned development of a unique and highly satisfactory character.[6]

This tradition had been largely lost in the United States by the middle of the nineteenth century. Since then the creation of planned new towns on public land has been almost entirely confined to the three Greenbelt towns of the 1930s and such government enterprise towns as Oak Ridge and Los Alamos. On the other hand, there have been a number of examples of large-scale planned urban developments built on privately owned land, most of it laboriously and secretively put together piece by piece: Columbia, Maryland, Reston, Virginia, and the Irvine Ranch in California—rare examples of large tracts already existing in rapidly urbanizing areas.

But large-scale public acquisition of land to facilitate development is not unknown in the United States. The concept has been used with irrigation projects, in which land in a benefit area is acquired as dry land and then resold as irrigable land, at advanced prices, after construction of the irrigation system. Among the advantages of the procedure is the fact that land-value increases are readily captured by government, which can use them to meet construction and other costs.

Recent Interest

Strong influences in the country are now pressing toward the resumption of public responsibility for urban development. This takes the form of, among other things, advance acquisition of areas critical to orderly growth. Thus the American Society of Planning Officials has recommended, "Local governments should be empowered to intervene directly in the development process by purchasing or condemning land [several years in advance of urbanization] and reselling or leasing it to private developers subject to conditions."[7]

The National Commission on Urban Problems (Douglas Commission),

> . . . believes that the time has come for government to assert its legitimate concerns with urban development through the use of techniques necessary

6 *Ibid.*, pp. 40 and 41.
7 American Society of Planning Officials, Report No. 250, 1969.

to accomplish public objectives. In many situations, this requires that the government actually obtain land—through purchase or eminent domain—and that regulation be supplemented by compensation to private property owners. Where actual purchase will result in the government's recapturing increases in land values for the public, government should deem this a legitimate function and an added incentive for direct action.[8]

The Commission recommended that state governments enact legislation enabling state and/or local development authorities or agencies or general-purpose governments to acquire land in advance of development for the following purposes: (a) to assure the continuing availability of sites for development; (b) to control the timing, location, type, and scale of development; (c) to prevent urban sprawl; and (d) to reserve for the public gains in land values resulting from the action of government in promoting and servicing development. At a minimum, such legislation should authorize the acquisition of land surrounding highway exchanges.

The Advisory Commission of Intergovernmental Relations has recommended

> . . . the establishment of state land development agencies in part to undertake large-scale urban and new communities land purchase, assembly, and improvement . . . [in part to] (1) acquire land by negotiation and through the exercise of eminent domain; (2) arrange for site development . . . (3) hold land for later use; (4) sell, lease or otherwise dispose of land . . . to private developers or public agencies.[9]

A task force of the American Institute of Architects in 1972 suggested there be development agencies with the power of eminent domain for acquisition of land and vacant and quasi-vacant areas, deteriorating areas, land in the path of development, and raw land at the periphery of metropolitan areas.[10]

The task force report sponsored by the Rockefeller Brothers Fund suggested

> . . . that governmental action be directed through new state agencies charged to assist and encourage desired development (especially large-scale development) and even to undertake it themselves. The agencies should . . . have a full range of powers to deal with problems of land assembly as well as those of utilities, regulations, financing, and other needs.[11]

The political process is also beginning to initiate change. State governments are becoming more involved in local planning and development, though this does not necessarily imply power to buy and sell land in the

---

8 Commission Report, "Building the American City," GPO, 1968, p. 250.

9 ACIR, *Urban and Rural America; Policies for Future Growth*, 1968, p. 161.

10 AIA, "A Plan for Urban Growth: Report of the National Policy Task Force," 1972, p. 10.

11 *The Use of Land, A Citizens' Policy Guide to Urban Growth*, 1973, p. 257.

context of improved land use of a general (rather than specific purpose) variety. Cases where it does include the financing of land acquisition are in Hawaii, Massachusetts (for low-income housing), and particularly New York State in which the New York State Urban Development Corporation is currently involved in extensive land acquisition and de facto land banking (it does not conceive itself a public land bank). In 1973 the Corporation owned outright $50 million of land and held several million more in leases and options.

The New York Regional Plan Association has advocated concentrating future growth in regional subcenters, whose nuclei would be already existing towns and cities.

> There is general agreement on a basic pattern of growth that maximizes urban benefits while minimizing rural invasion: discipline the urban growth within clearly-defined borders. Particularly, cluster the major office jobs, higher education, health complexes, department and specialty stores, reference libraries and government services in a few centers. These centers can grow large enough, then, to support high quality services, public transportation and efficient interchange among unrelated activities.

> If these clusters of large facilities are located in or near the center of existing urban areas, growth will strengthen the older places—such as Poughkeepsie, Newburgh, Kingston and Beacon. If, instead, the new is allowed to filter out along the highways and onto broad campuses, existing urban places will decline—as, indeed, some in the Mid-Hudson have been doing.[12]

To achieve this objective, the Regional Plan Association advocates several measures involving public acquisition of land in order to guide development along desired lines. Thus:

—The Urban Development Corporation should assemble land in centers that are underused and make it available for office construction at a favorable cost. The area should not have to be "blighted" to qualify.

—The Urban Development Corporation should organize and bear the "front-end" costs of the wholly new communities near Brewster, around New Paltz and, possibly, near Harriman. It should also be responsible for construction of the recommended planned-unit development neighborhoods around existing urban areas—40,000 to 60,000 units in all.

Such measures, calling for a temporary acquisition of land to guide the development of residential and commercial facilities, are in addition to those previously mentioned for acquiring 25 percent of the region's land for permanent parks and open space.

Suggested strategies for guiding regional development involve a number of other ventures as well—tax policies, transportation policies, zoning, strategic location of state and state-aided facilities (including community

---

12 Regional Plan Association and Mid-Hudson Pattern for Progress, *The Mid-Hudson: A Development Guide* (1973) p. 7.

colleges, libraries, hospitals, and art centers), location of sewer and water facilities, and other measures. Finally, "the state should establish a land bank in advance of highway and other developmental needs, in accordance with the plan. A revolving fund could be inaugurated with money from the sale of state-owned land that is not needed."

Specific Potential Advantages

The case for planning rests essentially on the faith that deliberative, thoughtful effort to define and achieve purposes will produce a better result than will uncoordinated behavior, subject only to fragmented controls and requirements now exercised by American communities. The relationship between advance acquisition of land and plans for an area is two-way. Acquisition must be related to notions about desirable directions and conditions necessary to achieve good development. In turn, large-scale land assembly under public auspices can do much to enhance the credibility and effectiveness of large-scale urban development planning.

We look next at specific objectives of the planning process, and at ways in which land banking may facilitate their achievement.

VALUES PROMOTED BY PLANNED DEVELOPMENT

Economic Efficiency—This is served by arranging activity centers—residences, employment centers, shopping, schools, recreation areas, and the rest—so as to minimize transportation needs with respect to distance. One dimension of good transportation planning involves ascertaining the purposes which each mode can serve most effectively; another involves principles of efficient local circulation of people and vehicles such as were introduced in Radburn, New Jersey, forty years ago; still another dimension involves an adequate supply of, and easy access to, recreational facilities. Of course, people will not necessarily use facilities in the way in which designers intend. Thus the English new towns early discovered that their attempts to achieve transportation economy by balancing the number of residents in the labor force with the number of jobs in the town was defeated by cross-commuting. The same phenomenon is apparent in Columbia today.

Beneficial Choice of Locations—In well-planned metropolitan areas the location of private business facilities, such as shopping, banks, central offices, etc., is determined with reference to the convenience of the user and the location of other activity centers. In the same way, factories and ancillary buildings are located in relation to labor supply and the impact of the facility on the neighborhood.

Reduction of Windfalls and Wipe-outs—As Hagman's chapter points out, public acquisition of land would reduce the extent to which private owners become the fortuitous victims or beneficiaries of zoning decisions and other government or private actions which affect the value of different land parcels in varying degrees.

Reducing the Cost of Government by Improved Siting and Reduction of the Purchase Price of Public Buildings—Advance acquisition tends to improve the likelihood of getting the best locations, and lowering the price relative to what might be charged when the need matures. This is an important element for all sorts of public buildings including schools, government offices and facilities.[13]

Reducing the Cost of Public Services (Roads, Sewers, and Other Utilities)—Advance acquisition can achieve more compact urban growth (no leapfrogging, etc.) and provide better choice of specific sites for these facilities at a lower cost.

Possible Reduction in the Net Cost of Government Through Capturing Increased Land Values for Public Purposes—One of the frequently mentioned potential advantages of public land banking is the possibility of capturing for public purposes land values which would otherwise accrue as unearned capital gains to private landholders. Such gains may take the form of money revenues from selling or leasing land for more than its acquisition, development, and carrying costs. They may also take the form of more generous apportionments of land for public purposes than would be feasible in the absence of land banking. In other words, the more narrowly economic gains from land banking ordinarily will be expected to take the form of larger parks and playgrounds, wider streets, etc., than would be feasible if such amenities had to be financed entirely by conventional taxes.

Reducing the Price of Developed Land—Another advantage often has to do with making land available for residential or other development at lower prices. As elsewhere noted, there may be such advantage with respect to land reserved for public purposes. With respect to land which will be used by the private sector, however, the government's main purpose is to facilitate planning not to reduce the costs of land to private developers below its market level (taking "market level" as the amounts that could be obtained by selling land at public auction). Should the government sell for less than its market level, the purchasers can reap windfall profits either through quick resale or in the normal course of development. Private enrichment through the resale of lands acquired from government agencies at less than market value has been a common source of corruption in the United States. The problem of windfall profits has arisen also in other countries which have attempted, through land-banking programs, to reduce the costs of land made available for private development.

[13] Shoup and Mack, *op. cit.*

Land-banking programs should emphasize capturing land value increments for public use not on providing cheap land for private development. Where it is desired to subsidize certain types of development, such as low-income housing, land may be made available at less-than-market figures, but in such cases (1) the government should prevent resale of the land for windfall profits, and (2) the difference between the market price and the figure at which the land is made available—i.e., the amount of the implicit subsidy—should be shown on the books as a welfare-category expenditure.

ADVANTAGES BEARING ON THE QUALITATIVE AND QUANTITATIVE ADEQUACY OF LAND FOR PRIVATE PURPOSES, AS DETERMINED BY NONMARKET AND MARKET CRITERIA

Aesthetic Quality—This is a subjective concept. Nearly everyone accepts the notion that factories should not be in residential areas, and few would want to live across the street from a junk yard. (Harlem residents have been agitated for years about the location of a sewage treatment center on Manhattan's upper West Side.) But while there is general agreement that the well-planned community avoids unseemly sights, sounds, and smells, there is less agreement on the use of green space and plantings, buildings and neighborhood design, circulation facilities, and other values put forward by architects and urban designers. Trying to improve urban design is something like trying to raise the level of television programs.

Environmental Quality—Somewhere between economics and aesthetics, and partaking of both, are the aspects of environmental quality having to do with unpolluted air, swimmable water, preservation of green space in the interest of climatic control as well as visual pleasure, play and so on. Since these attributes tend to be space-intensive, advance land acquisition is an important tool in the planning kit.

CORRECTING SOCIAL INEQUITIES RESULTING FROM PRIVATE MARKET FORCES

Land for Low-income Housing—The failure of the present market-oriented system to provide land for low-income housing is not exclusively a market failure, of course, since the market is reinforced by many kinds of controls and restrictions. The mere allocation of land from a land bank for low-income housing does not mean that neighbors will happily accept low-income housing or that the market for middle- and upper-income housing will be unaffected, or the low-income families will be greatly benefited. Still, deliberate planning for an equitable allocation of housing space on government-owned land could hardly avoid achieving better results than have been produced by the existing mechanism, if for no other reason than that the planning presumably would be done by an agency with regional perspective. However, this is certainly an example of the need to include a land bank as one tool in a policy kit.

INCREASING THE POTENTIAL OF URBAN DEVELOPMENT PLANNING

In addition to improving land use and spatial relationships, land banking may enlarge the entire planning perspective and generate new planning concepts, as in the Stockholm case.

Financial Dimensions

We next consider financial benefits and costs. Of particular interest is the question of whether land banking programs can ordinarily capture for public purposes the increases in land value which accrue as land is converted from agricultural (or other non-urban) uses to urban uses, and which would otherwise show up as capital gains to private landowners. There are several possibilities.

First, public acquisition and disposal, through sale or lease, of land in developing areas can provide substantial revenues which in many ways are preferable to conventional taxes. Similarly, governments may save money in the long run by advance acquisition of land for public purposes.

Second, land acquired and held for long periods may be a losing proposition, in that acquisition costs and carrying charges may exceed the amounts which governments may realize (or save) through land banking programs. But this does not necessarily negate the desirability of land banking; it may be desirable by reason of other advantages such as better planning.

Third, potential benefits may be dissipated by poor management and political hanky-panky which drain off gains into private pockets. After all, land deals have always been one of the larger objects of corruption in American politics.

Fourth, mere public ownership of land does not ensure that land will be put to the best use. Internecine conflicts among government agencies, for example between highway and park departments, may be expected to continue. Economic development agencies will argue with conservation agencies as to the extent to which industry should be allowed to pollute, just as they do today—and just as they do in the Soviet, where the government claims to own all the land.

But having noted the hazards to effective land policy implicit in the last two points above, we will return to the narrowly financial aspects of land banking.

POTENTIAL ECONOMIC GAINS

These have to do with advantages to government in acquiring land before its value has risen to reflect fully impending conversion to urban uses. If values of land increase at a rate higher than the cost of acquiring, improving, and holding it, governments can gain by land banking. The converse also holds.

The size of potential gain depends on:

1. The price initially paid for the land and the extent to which acquisition raises the price above the level which would have otherwise obtained.
2. The rate of interest paid by the government agency to finance acquisition.
3. The amount of taxes foregone (whether or not the purchasing government is the jurisdiction which imposes property taxes), including those on any improvements which might have been erected on the land.
4. Costs of improvements made to the land while in government ownership.
5. The administrative costs of acquiring land, managing it, and ultimately disposing of it.

From these costs must be deducted any revenue from the land while it is held in the bank.

The final gain or loss is the amount for which the public agency disposes of banked land. For land converted to public purposes it is the cost of acquiring such land in the absence of land banking, minus accumulated net costs (interest, foregone taxes, improvements and administration, minus the accumulated value of incidental revenues).

Acquisition Costs—There is a quantum difference between the value of land in agricultural use and its value in urban use. In general, the latter value is a function of density of use. Theoretically, the price of agricultural land which will some day be converted to urban use is the discounted value of the land after conversion. Presumptively, the higher the discount rate, the greater is the uncertainty of the occurrence and nature of the conversion and its timing. For private developers, the discount rate must include a margin for the assumption of such risks. A public agency able to exert a measure of control over land uses and timing of development faces less risk and thereby can use a lower discount rate.

It is often assumed that substantial public purchases will raise the price of other land in the area by decreasing the supply. This assumption overlooks several factors which may have effects to the contrary.

—If purchases are made in a quiet market (long before expected urban development), they should have relatively little effect on the price of lands used primarily for agricultural purposes. The effect probably will be the greater on active developments already under way.
—The existence of public land, which ultimately will be released for development, will limit the prices which developers are willing to pay for other land, the more so if the public agency follows the policy of timing land sales so as to keep prices down.

If increases do threaten, the government agency concerned could write suitable legislation to protect itself against such induced increases by devices such as that employed in Puerto Rico or by exercising the power of eminent domain.

Foregone Taxes—Land held by government agencies ordinarily is not subject to property taxes, though if the land-banking agency is other than the one imposing property taxes it may make payments in lieu of taxes, which constitute a cost. Any net reduction of taxes collected, relative to what would have been collected had land remained in private ownership, is of course a cost to the taxing government.

If acquisition for a land bank causes increases in prices of land outside the bank, and if tax assessors are prompt in putting such increases on the tax rolls, there will be some offset to the taxes foregone on the banked land. Similarly, taxable improvements which otherwise would have been made on the banked land may be erected on nonbanked land, in which case they are not lost to the tax rolls.

Interest Costs—These are usually calculated with reference to the rates on obligations of the public agency concerned. In the United States, state and local government obligations are usually somewhat lower than rates on comparable other obligations by virtue of exemption of interest from federal income tax. (The exemption has been withdrawn from certain bonds issued to finance industrial development, however.)

To put these annual cost figures in some rough setting, we observe that interest rates of tax-exempt obligations are running between 5 and 6 percent. Tax rates on undeveloped land, which is generally underassessed, probably seldom exceed 2 percent, and in most areas are considerably less. Adding the two high figures gives a carrying cost of 8 percent for these two costs, which are the main time-related factors in a land banking operation.

DATA ON LAND VALUE INCREASES

There has been no experience in the United States with large-scale land banks. The paucity of data respecting land values and prices at various stages of land-use development, and the widely differing conditions under which land banks may operate, preclude generalizations as to their likely profitability, judged by banking criteria. The following data, less than comprehensive, are about as far as analysts have been willing to go for periods prior to the recent acceleration in the pace of inflation.

1. Studies of land value increases during the 1950s and 1960s indicate an average rate of increase of urban land prices, as represented by prices of vacant lots, of well under 10 percent. The same was true of the average annual increase in the value of farmland in metropolitan counties; the unweighted average annual increase in 29 states between 1954 and 1965

was approximately 6 percent, and in only one state, Maryland, did the figure exceed 10 percent (10.8).[14]

On the average it appears that the game of holding land for speculative increases would have been a losing one, since the increase rate usually failed to match combined interest and tax rates. On the other hand, state and municipal governments in several of the 29 states cited in the survey could have at least broken even in that the average increase of metropolitan farmland values was high enough to offset the costs of borrowing on tax-exempt obligations plus foregone property taxes.

2. It is generally agreed that the quantum jump in urban land prices occurs during the process of converting land from agricultural to urban use. Speculative increases in farmland values, which raise the price of farmland above its value in agricultural use, commonly occur before— sometimes many years before—actual conversion. Thus the above-cited study of farmland values in metropolitan and nonmetropolitan counties found that the price per acre of farmland in metropolitan counties averaged more than 50 percent more than land prices in nonmetropolitan counties.

Data cited by Schmid indicate an average increase in the sale price of developed lots (minus development costs) over farmland of approximately eleven-fold.[15] This corresponds to Maisel's finding that building site prices even on the suburban fringe were 10 or more times agricultural land prices. Prices in different areas on the metropolitan fringe of course differ substantially, depending on numerous factors, which include distance from the central city or other high-density centers, accessibility to transportation and such other facilities as water and sewer lines, and the topography of the area. Zoning is a critical factor—tracts zoned for industrial and commercial uses customarily command much higher prices than do lands zoned for rural residence. In the Philadelphia area, for instance, land appropriate for filling stations was selling at one time for the equivalent of $100,000 an acre while other land in the same area was selling for $2,000–$3,000 an acre.

The proportion of the quantum jump in land values that can be recovered by a public land-bank operation, however, depends on (in addition to the above-mentioned factors) when the land bank arrives on the scene, the primary and secondary impacts of its own land-acquisition operations, and the length of time it must hold land prior to conversion.

Land banking may be most profitable when land is acquired far in advance of expected development. Where condemnation is involved, such a degree of business prudence is likely to be resisted by the courts, which

---

[14] Source: Grace Milgram, *Urban Land Prices—Directions and Dynamics,* National Commission on Urban Problems, Research Report No. 13 (GPO, 1968), p. 34.

[15] A. Allen Schmid, *Converting Land from Rural to Urban Uses,* Resources for the Future, 1968, p. 26.

like to see land acquired for public purposes actually put to its intended use with reasonable celerity, measured in years rather than decades. And it certainly runs counter to prevailing public sentiment, which has regarded land and land-holding and profiting therefrom, as a private rather than a public prerogative.

Table 1 indicates the magnitudes of land-value increases necessary to offset various annual cost rates of holding land.

TABLE 1. ACCUMULATED COSTS OF HOLDING BANKED LAND

Annual Cost Rate (Percent)*	Accumulated Costs of Land Holdings, Percentage of Original Cost (Years)			
	5	10	20	30
4	122	148	219	324
6	134	179	321	574
8	147	216	466	1006
12	176	310	965	2995

* Net annual costs divided by purchase cost.

If the net cost, for example, were 4 percent per year, and land were held for five years, the total cost of holding would be 22 percent of the purchase price, and land-value increases exceeding 22 percent would produce a profit. With a 4 percent annual cost and a holding period of 30 years, the breakeven increase is 224 percent. With an annual cost rate of 12 percent, however, the breakeven increase for five years is 76 percent, and for 30 years is 2895 percent, or nearly 30 times the original cost of the land.

The figures, combined with data on land value increase cited above, dramatize the point that any possibility of realizing substantial revenues from land banking depends largely upon the annual cost of holding land and the length of time it must be held.

The table shows, for example, that if, as noted above, the value of urban land is eleven times that of farm land, a land bank operation would gain substantially with annual carrying charges of 8 percent and a holding period of 20 years; it would still gain if the holding period were 30 years. With annual carrying costs of 12 percent and a holding period of 20 years, the operation would approximately break even. With a 30 year holding period, it would lose.

BENEFIT-COST RATIOS

How do benefits contrast with costs? This question appears not to be asked as routinely of land banking as of other government investments where favorable benefit-cost ratios (often defined as a ratio of one or greater) are the accepted criterion.

The reason is apparent from considering benefits listed in preceding sections: many of them concern aspects of the "quality of life" which are not readily measurable in dollars. "Social indicators" recognize many of them, but no way has been devised of incorporating them into a system for purposes of social decision-making.

In the meantime, it would seem that some types of clearly identifiable benefits can be formally recognized; others can perhaps at least tip the scales in marginal cases. An obvious example of the former group is the subsidy involved in selling land for low-income housing at substantially less than cost—a benefit which can be measured as the difference between the market price and the subsidized price of land. (The amount of the subsidy should be charged to a welfare or human development account rather than being shown as a deduction from revenues of the land bank.)

Land banking may largely be viewed as a means of internalizing the cost of improved public amenities associated with "good" land-use planning, which otherwise would have to be paid for from general tax revenues or foregone altogether.

There is no reason in principle why some such costs cannot be internalized by a private development organization which could assemble land for new town or PUD sites at rural land prices, manage land development activities of single projects, and control and coordinate the growth and development of the new communities. It is argued that a new town or PUD private developer would have ample incentives to provide amenities such as parkland and recreation facilities, along with shopping and entertainment, because he receives all the advantages of increased land values and/or more rapid land sales which these things would generate. Small developers, on the other hand, have little incentive to pay the costs of providing public amenities when part of the benefits which accrue therefrom, in the form of increased land values, may go to neighboring developers or landowners. Something like this has been happening in the development of larger-scale planned new towns and the more numerous PUDs. On the other hand, this type of development is still the exception rather than the rule. Even the provision for financial assistance to private enterprise for large-scale land assembly and development (under Title VII of the Housing and Urban Development Act of 1970) thus far has had little impact.

With respect to infrastructure and urban amenities many local jurisdictions have been requiring that such facilities be provided by developers, as a condition for obtaining subdivision and building permits. A New Jersey court, however, has recently ruled that municipalities cannot legally require developers to supply land for recreational purposes. If this decision were widely followed, urban development practices would be set back even further, which in turn would strengthen the case for public land banking.

MAJOR OBSTACLES

The major obstacles to land banking in the United States are organizational and political.

Land banking is a highly complex undertaking which is dependent on integration with a comprehensive, flexible mechanism for planning and guiding urban growth.[16] Few agencies of metropolitan scale or larger are equipped with jurisdictional authority or organizational capacity to operate a land bank. (New York State's Urban Development Corporation is usually cited as an exception.) As for potential acceptability, the action of February, 1974, by the House of Representatives apparently rejecting a comparatively modest federal land-use bill (already approved by the Senate) indicated that nationally, and probably in most states and metropolitan areas, public support for large-scale land acquisition for urban development (a much more drastic measure than anything in the federal land-use bill) has still to materialize. Moreover, it is opposed by a formidable set of private landowners, land developers, and their cohorts of the real estate lobby.

It is at these levels of organizational and administrative capability that the viability of land banking will meet its real test. Is there any hope, then, of its becoming a significant tool? Fortunately, the answer is yes. It is possible to proceed with a variety of situations that are favorable to advanced land acquisition ventures. What is learned in these situations can later be applied to more difficult ones. Consider some possibilities.

Special-purpose advance land acquisition is already a well established technique for providing for expected future needs. A survey of members of the National League of Cities in 1966 suggested that perhaps 30 percent of cities of over 50,000 inhabitants engaged in some sort of advance acquisition, though typically of limited scope. Parks and schools were the most usual purpose.[17] Another type which has been advocated but not yet realized enlarges on the growing interest in nonstructural flood management. Advance acquisition of undeveloped floodplains could provide a way of controlling the use of the land and thereby capitalize on the tactic of getting people away from flood waters rather than getting flood waters away from people. The numerous instances of municipal acquisition of land for industrial development are another precedent.

These ventures afford experience in the acquisition and disposal of sites

16 A useful discussion of needed measures appears in Marion Clawson's *Suburban Land Conversion in the United States: An Economic and Governmental Process* published for Resources for the Future, Inc. by the Johns Hopkins Press, Baltimore and London, 1971, Ch. 17.

17 Shoup and Mack, *op. cit.*, Ch. II.

and opportunities for cooperation among various governments and among city agencies in formulating and implementing development plans —all of which are important to any broad-scale land banking effort.[18]

Land banks may be able to use, as initial "capital," sites already acquired. The Land Law Review Commission recommended the use of some government holdings of forest or open space for satellite cities. Tax default lands within towns are further possible examples. Another possibility lies in the use of excess condemnation along highway routes and particularly at highway intersections to keep control over the highly dynamic development characteristic of such areas.

FINANCING

Financing land banking is a subject in itself. We will observe only that most recent proponents of land banking have looked to the federal government as a prime source of financial support. Charles Haar and others have suggested creation of an Urban Bank (Urbank) to complement, by helping finance, urban land banks. In the last analysis, however, what is needed is a means of providing funds to meet substantial front-end load costs and the slow return of capital which deters private developers.[19] The English model, wherein the U. K. Treasury provided development funds at low rates of interest to new-town development authorities which pay back the loans through proceeds of land leases and sales, may offer useful precedents.

The fact that land in developing areas and in periods of inflation is an appreciating asset, distinguishes it from other capital assets purchased by governments which depreciate over time. This important contrast suggests that governments contemplating land-banking need financial instruments designed specifically to take account of the crucial difference between land and other capital assets.

A NEW TECHNIQUE OF FINANCING LAND ACQUISITION FOR SPECIFIC PURPOSES

First, given the continuing and accelerating inflation in urban land values, land usually is cheaper the earlier it is acquired.

Second, once land has been privately developed, its use for many public purposes is foreclosed entirely, or it can be reconverted from private to public use only at great expense. Cases abound of towns impoverished of

[18] *Toward an Understanding of General Land Banking at the Metropolitan Scale*, Harvey Flechner; a dissertation submitted to the faculty of the School of Engineering and Architecture of the Catholic University of America, August 1973, Washington, D. C., pp. 118–125.

[19] The furthest advance thus far has been Title VII of the Housing and Urban Development Act of 1970, which provided a battery of financing tools—grants, loans and loan guarantees, primarily to assist private developers undertaking large-scale land assembly.

land to use for parks, school sites, and open space because they did not think of the future when land was still available.

The irony is that acquiring and holding land can be essentially a cost-less process for a public agency, and can even be very profitable. A municipality, by acquiring land in 1974 which it may need sometime in the future, can avoid paying an inflated price in the future (say in 1984). Or, if it later finds that the land is not needed after all, it can then dispose of the land at a profit.

Conventionally, municipal councils and their constituents do not look at the matter this way and tend to resist giving thought to public improvements until the need is urgent and present. The present generation of taxpayers is seldom much concerned with the welfare of future generations. They are usually reluctant to consider their own welfare some years later if such action would mean raising taxes now, even if by so doing they could avoid much greater increases in the future.

The reluctance of public bodies to plan for future land use may be overcome in part by new financing tools which would ease the immediate burden on hard-pressed municipal budgets. One possible device, which we have not seen mentioned elsewhere, is that of financing advance land acquisition through discount bonds instead of conventional interest-bearing bonds. With the discount bond, interest accrues over the life of the bond and is paid at maturity date. A municipality issuing discount bonds could thereby defer raising taxes to finance interest payments. To see how the process might work assume:

1. A land parcel of 100 acres, available at $100,000 in 1974.
2. Land values projected to rise at an annual rate of 10 percent, equivalent to a doubling of values in approximately 7.2 years.
3. A market discount rate (yield for which bonds can be sold) of 5.5 percent on 10-year bonds.

The municipality, to obtain $100,000 purchase funds, issues discount bonds due in 10 years, of a value of approximately $171,000 (equivalent to a yield of 5.5 percent). In 1984 the land will be worth approximately $240,000. The municipality then can decide whether (1) to retain all of the land for public purposes, (2) retain part of the land and sell the rest, or (3) to sell all the land.

If in 1984 the municipality decides to retain all the land, it can refinance the discount bonds on a more conventional basis, but the refinancing will require a new bond issue of only $171,000 compared to the $240,000 which would have been required had the municipality waited ten years to acquire the land (assuming it were still available).

Second, if the municipality decides to retain, say, half the land and sell the rest at the 1984 assumed market price ($120,000), it would need to refinance only the difference ($51,000) between the face value of the discount bonds and the sale price ($171,000 minus $120,000). If the municipality had to buy the land in 1984, the cost would be $120,000.

Third, if the municipality decides to dispose of the entire parcel in 1984, it can pay off the discount bonds from the sale price, leaving a gain of $51,000.

These computations take no account of the foregone taxes on the 100 acres of land. Since tax rates on the market value of undeveloped land are low (compared to rates on developed property) the loss would be relatively small, perhaps $10,000–$15,000 over the entire period.

Conventional municipal financial practice involves the establishment of a sinking fund and regular contributions thereto or serial bonds of staggered maturities which are paid off as they mature. Land is a quite different kind of asset in that its value tends to appreciate, thus eliminating the need for a sinking fund. Conventional instruments are designed primarily to finance depreciating assets, with at least a rough correspondence between the rate of depreciation and the rate of accumulation of sinking funds. In the case of a discount bond issued to finance a land purchase, the land itself could serve as stand-in for the sinking fund; the claim could be formalized by attaching a lien on the land to the bond issue, thus making it in effect a first mortgage bond.

We know of no precedent in state-local financing for this particular kind of arrangement; however, some states and municipalities have shown considerable ingenuity in working out new arrangements with private firms to finance plant construction. There should be no great technical difficulty in working out a discount bond arrangement. Constitutions or statutes of most states would have to be amended to permit it, but it would be possible under the New Jersey constitution and possibly others.

Probably the biggest obstacle would be a lack of a broad market for such an unusual type of municipal issue. We contemplate that bonds would be backed by the full faith and credit of the municipality. The only risk is that land prices will rise at a rate less than carrying costs or, at the extreme, that they would collapse. Given the various upward pressures on urban land prices and the virtual certainty that they will continue, the risk of land-price slowdown or collapse is remote. The risks of not acting promptly to acquire land which may be needed in the future are far greater.

Brian J. L. Berry

7

The Question of Policy Alternatives

> *He who lets the world, or his own portion of it,*
> *choose his plan of life for him, has no need of*
> *any other faculty than the ape-like one of imita-*
> *tion. He who chooses his plan for himself, em-*
> *ploys all his faculties. He must use observation to*
> *see, reason and judgment to foresee, activity to*
> *gather materials for decision, discrimination to*
> *decide, and when he has decided, firmness and*
> *self-control to hold to his deliberate decision.*
>
> John Stuart Mill,
> On Liberty, 1859

Sir Henry Maine pointed out over a century ago that one of the essential ingredients in the emergence of modern urban-industrial society was a change in the concept of land ownership. Originally held in common by traditional social groups, land has been transformed into another exchangeable commodity with price determined by competition among prospective users.

However, the value of land is not the value of the physical object; it is the value of the bundle of rights associated with property ownership. The exchange of a piece of land involves the transfer of these rights from one individual to another. The rights are significant because they help a man form expectations which he can reasonably hold in his dealings with others—expectations that find expression in laws, customs, and mores of

BRIAN J. L. BERRY, *the Irving B. Harris Professor of Urban Geography at the University of Chicago, is Director of Training Programs at the university's Center for Urban Studies. Dr. Berry has written numerous books and articles on urban affairs and has an active extra-university involvement in urban and regional planning.*

society. An owner expects the community to protect his rights—including the right to benefit or harm himself or others—and to permit him to act in those ways not prohibited by the rights.

The right to benefit or harm others and its complement, to be benefited or harmed by others, is important because it involves *externalities*—the effects of each land user's activities on others—and their *internalization*—how the effects are accounted for in land prices and land use. An individual land owner will try to maximize present value by assessing the future time streams of costs and benefits associated with alternative land uses, selecting that use which he believes will maximize present value. In doing so, he will take into account the benefits conveyed to him by others and the costs imposed on him by others, but not the converse.

Thus, in any well-functioning competitive land market, the price of each piece of property should reflect the present value of the future stream of net benefits expected to flow over the useful life of the "highest and best" improvements, i.e., those land uses that maximize net returns. This generalization is, however, subject to the workings of time. Many capital investments cannot be changed overnight. A commitment to a particular land use may therefore be a commitment for several decades, and one which is fixed rather than mobile. Where major capital investments are involved, it will only be in the *new* property market that one sees "highest and best" uses being established at any point in time; elsewhere the toll that depreciation takes of fixed capital investments before their economically useful life has run out will be apparent.

As noted, the value of any site will be enhanced by benefits conveyed by others (i.e., positive externalities, such as a "good neighborhood" and a "fine school district" or "excellent accessibility"). Likewise, the value of a site will be reduced by costs imposed by others (e.g., negative externalities such as air pollution or the swath of noise associated with airport landing patterns). The private property market thus produces an "internalization" of many externalities. A would-be land owner must pay more to occupy and use a site well-endowed with positive externalities, while he will be far less willing to pay for property which bears a heavy burden of negative externalities.

One result is land uses that are patterned geographically because the purchase or rental of the physical commodity, land, conveys the exclusive right to occupy a particular *location* and to use a particular set of *site amenities*. One thus can distinguish between the *locational value* and the *amenity value* of the property. Both are relative values, in that they involve interdependencies and reflect externalities.

Locational value is determined by relative accessibility to the activity centers that serve as points of focus within any spatial organization, the lines and channels of movement to and from these centers, and the identifiable neighborhoods, communities, districts and regions that are the essence of human territoriality. At any time these are a matter of inherited spatial organization, although they will be affected by both public and private decisions. But since different uses have different needs for access to different things, the result is a mix of competing uses that varies from one location to another. Therefore, both land use and land value vary systematically with relative location, a product of the desire to be as close as possible to certain things to benefit from their positive spillovers, and as far away as possible from others, to avoid the negative externalities.

Amenity value is in part a matter of the relative worth to prospective users of the physical attributes of the site, such as a waterfront location, and in part also a matter of the acquired social attributes of the site, such as neighborhood quality. Again, both land use and land value vary systematically with the relative worth of the amenities. Those best able to pay will preempt the better endowed sites and will relegate to those least able to compete the least desirable sites in the least desirable locations.

The problem is that this classical theory of land use is built on the presumption that virtually everything of significant value is suitable for private ownership. The competitive market is visualized as a mechanism through which mutual gains can be maximized by individual negotiation and choices. But it is now being argued, not only that the pure private property concept applies satisfactorily to a narrowing range of natural resources and economic activities, but that because externalities have not been properly internalized, mutual gains have not been maximized. Within the American planning fraternity and among the nation's ecoactivists one sees and hears in common usage such expletives as "slurbs," and pejoratives such as "urban sprawl" and "spread city." "Megalopolis" is perceived to be the ultimate aberration, a case of hydrocephalous gigantism about to strangle in its own effluents. Dispersion and decentralization are treated, axiomatically, as inefficient. Land is said to be polluted.

The essence of the charge is that the individualized nature of the traditional land-use decision permits neither environmental relationships nor social justice to be taken into account short of impending disaster. Left unaccounted, the "crisis ghetto" into which our social effluents are discarded is, it is asserted, boiling over as crime rates escalate and abandonment increases, thereby threatening the basis of prosperity and freedom in society as a whole. Equally, the wholesale discarding of physical and chemical effluents into air and water and on land ignores the complex interdependencies that exist between nature and culture in ecosystems. There are losses in wellbeing, and again the basis of prosperity and even of life itself *is said to be* threatened, because ultimately the piper must be paid.

Ignoring the histrionics of many of the charges, two important points are being made. One issue relates the impact of "externalities" and whether policy alternatives might provide for their "internalizing." The second relates to common property resources—those impossible to be assigned private property rights, where lack of a proper pricing mechanism produces misallocations. Goods formerly free, including air and water, have become scarce, but the market has not properly assigned them prices because they are in a crucial respect common property. Thus intervention of some kind is required. The question is: What sort of intervention? What sort of policymaking is required, and what sort of policies?

Policy Alternatives

There are four frequently-overlapping but clearly distinguishable policymaking styles. Each asks different questions, and produces different results. The question is whether any of these represents a viable policymaking alternative to the traditional mode of land-use determination in the United States.

Alternative, and perhaps more meaningful, labels for the four styles than those used to describe them somewhat whimsically in the columns of Table 1 are, respectively:

  a. crisis intervention planning,
  b. regulatory planning,
  c. entrepreneurial planning,
  d. cybernetic or systems planning.

Crisis-intervention planning is exactly what the name suggests: "firefighting." A problem is perceived by some interest-group to exist and to be profound enough to demand action. The location, nature and intensity of the problem are assessed and an ameliorative action is devised. The underlying philosophy is that decisions, actions and change are a matter of the free choices and interactions of individuals within society, and the proper governmental role is the minimal one of attending to those unfortunate negative externalities that go beyond individuals' abilities or willingness to effect a private cure. Thus, slums must be cleared, traffic congestion ameliorated, criminals incarcerated, fires extinguished, and pollution abated. The governmental role is forever secondary, responding to forces that have played themselves out in the past. Moreover, while the nostrum may cure the immediate ill, its long-term effects on present and future decisions remain largely unknown, producing "windfalls" and "wipeouts" outside the realm of governmental decision-making.

Regulatory planning attempts to take one step beyond crisis intervention by so influencing contemporary decisions, actions, and trends as to avoid problems in the future. Thus, the body of law helps define and protect the bundle of rights endowed by property ownership, and forbids certain kinds of behavior that would likely result in problems in the future. To cite one example, building codes are intended to reduce the risk

TABLE I. FOUR POLICYMAKING STYLES

	Planning for Present Concerns	Planning for the Future		Planning for the Future
	Reacting to Past Problems	Responding to Predicted Futures		Creating Desired Future
	Ameliorative Problem-Solving	Allocative Trend-Modifying	Exploitive Opportunity-Seeking	Normative Goal-Oriented
	Planning for the Present	Planning toward the Future	Planning with the Future	Planning from the Future
PLANNING MODE	Analyze problems, design interventions, allocate resources accordingly.	Determine and make the *best* of trends and allocate resources in accordance with desires to promote or alter them.	Determine and make the *most* of trends and allocate resources so as to take advantage of what is to come.	Decide on the *future desired* and allocate resources so that trends are changed or created accordingly. Desired future may be based on present, predicted or new values.
"PRESENT" OR SHORT RANGE RESULTS	*Ameliorate Present Problems*	*A Sense of Hope* New allocations shift activities	*A Sense of Triumphing Over Fate* New allocations shift activities	*A Sense of Creating Destiny* New allocations shift activities
"FUTURE" OR LONG RANGE RESULTS OF ACTIONS	*Haphazardly Modify the Future* by reducing the future burden and sequelae of present problems	*Gently Balance and Modify the Future* by avoiding predicted problems and achieving a "balanced" progress to avoid creating major bottlenecks and new problems.	*Unbalance and Modify the Future* by taking advantage of predicted happenings, avoiding some problems and cashing in on others without major concern for emergence of new problems.	*Extensively Modify the Future* by aiming for what could be "Change the predictions" by changing values or goals, match outcomes to desires, avoid or change problems to ones easier to handle or tolerate.

of fire and seek to maintain sound and healthful structures; similarly, subdivision regulations seek to maintain orderly site designs. The essence of this planning style is conservative—the maintenance of existing "mainstream" values, while obeying the adage that "an ounce of prevention is worth a pound of cure."

Entrepreneurial planning is more common in the private than the public arena, because businesses have longer time perspectives than politicians. Whereas the regulatory planner seeks to analyze the causes of change so as to predict likely future problems and to identify points of intervention that, if utilized, can prevent the occurrence of the predicted problems, the entrepreneurial planner analyzes change and projects it into the future to see where new growth opportunities may exist as much as a generation ahead. Instead of planning regulations that preserve the essence of the mainstream on into the future, he plans speculative actions that will realize the latent growth potentials, frequently changing the directions of change as a result. Thus, real estate investors, responding to the market opportunities perceived to be latent in postwar suburbanization, devised the planned shopping center as a realization instrument. As a consequence they transformed the entire retail structure of metropolitan America.

The final policymaking mode involves the use of cybernetic rationality and systems planning. Future goals are set, and the system is analyzed to determine the instrumentalities that may be used to steer the system toward the goals, to monitor progress, and to adjust direction if there is a veering off course. For this type of planning to be successful, power must be centralized, control must be assured, and means-ends closure must be obtained. Thus, public ownership of the land was essential for Sweden to develop a radically different land-use pattern for Stockholm. Given such control capability, if it is determined that the present system is inherently incapable of achieving the goals, the resulting recommendation may be a radical one—change the system itself so that it is conformal to the goals set!

If crisis intervention is forever past-oriented, and regulatory and entrepreneurial policies plan toward a future that either ensures the present mainstream or realizes latent growth opportunities with unknown but substantial attendant transformations, cybernetic systems planning involves policies reconstructed backwards *from* a desired future state.

Policymaking—American Style

Let us return to the individualized mechanisms by which property values are derived and land uses determined in the United States and ask which of the four policymaking styles are most representative of American practice, and which represent viable alternatives if it is desired to produce significantly different land-use outcomes or to internalize those externalities that degrade the nation's community resources.

The traditional process of land-use determination involves *economizing*, a method by which scarce resources are best allocated among competing uses by individuals seeking to maximize their returns. Economizing is made possible by a market mechanism that serves as the arbiter, and prices that continually respond to shifts in demand and supply. As Daniel Bell observes in *The Coming of the Post-Industrial Society*, over the past hundred years, economics has developed a rigorous and elegant general system of theory to explain how this economizing mode works, used as it is in conditions of individualism, perfect information, and rational choice, with the good of the society asserted to be the summation of the individual utilities.

The words we associate with economizing are "maximization," "optimization," "least cost"—in short, the components of a conception of rationality that seems to be fully supportive of the Domestic Council's report on *National Growth, 1972* in which it was concluded that

> Patterns of growth are influenced by countless decisions made by individuals, families, and businesses. These decisions are aimed at achieving the personal goals of those who make them, and reflect healthy free choices in our society. Locational shifts by individuals reflect, in part, a search for better job opportunities or for a better climate, while businessmen relocate where they can operate most efficiently and therefore make the most profit . . . in a Nation that values freedom in the private sector and democratic choice in the public, these decisions themselves cannot be dictated.
>
> In many nations, the central government has undertaken forceful, comprehensive policies to control the process of growth. Similar policies have not been adopted in the United States for several reasons. Among the most important of these is the form of government . . . [which] preserves the ability of citizens to have a major voice in determining policies that directly affect them. . . . It is not feasible for the highest level of government to design policies for development that can operate successfully in all parts of the Nation.

The conception of rationality reflected here is, of course, a rationality of *means*. The ends of life themselves were never given; they were seen as multiple or varied, to be chosen freely by the members of society. Economics would seek to satisfy these choices in the "best way," i.e., the most efficient means possible in order to "maximize" satisfaction. This distinction between rational means and plurality of ends must be emphasized. American society has never felt the need to define its ends or to establish priorities within some set of ends. It has always eschewed such collective decision-making. The theoretical virtue of the market is that it supposedly coordinates human interdependence in some fashion better than any known alternatives, in accordance with the expressed preferences of buyers and sellers.

What ultimately provides direction for the economy, as Veblen pointed out long ago, is not the price system itself, however, but the *value system of the culture* in which the economy is embedded. To the extent that this value system permits a public planning role, it is a mixture of planning styles—to enhance the central values of the mainstream by curative programs and by regulatory mechanisms that prevent future mishaps, while keeping open the opportunities for entrepreneurial planning in the private arena. Thus, if there is to be an alternative, it is represented by the goal-oriented policymaking style, *provided that* we have the knowledge and capability to design relatively mistake-free "solutions."

This is not, of course, to say that the U. S. Government has not played and does not play a significant role in determining land use or affecting land-use decisions. Admittedly, on the surface this may appear so. Of the approximately 2.2 billion acres of land and water within the territory of the United States, Congress exercises original jurisdiction as to planning and regulation of land use over only 43,148 acres—the District of Columbia. Since authority over other land is not explicitly granted to Congress under the U. S. Constitution, the Tenth Amendment has long been considered to reserve such jurisdiction for the sovereign states. And by virtue of the nearly unanimous delegation of this power by each state, the effective power to plan and regulate the use of land in the United States lies with the lowest level of government, either municipal or county. And many have observed that the regulatory powers of local governments are most often used to support the private market interests of specific groups, rather than to change them.

There is, of course, now some tendency for the states to exercise land-use powers they had previously abdicated to local governments. This "quiet revolution" in land use includes New York's and California's system of development permits, Vermont's capital gains tax on land transactions, preferential assessments in Arkansas and Florida, deferred taxation in Maryland and Alaska, and contracts to avoid urbanization in exchange for lower property taxes in Hawaii and Pennsylvania.

But in spite of these efforts, the previous statement still stands. Yet the description of the federal role is obviously inadequate to characterize the actual importance of Congress in the determination of land use in the United States. For instance, the United States Government through various instrumentalities owns outright approximately 700 million acres or one-third of the nation's surface area. State and local policies fade into legal fictions in this largely undeveloped and remote land; the undisputed sovereign of the public domain is the federal government.

As to the other two-thirds of the nation's territory, the influence of Congress and more recently the Executive Branch in the determination of land use is far more profound and pervasive than the doctrine of state sovereignty would seem to admit. Much of this influence historically has been exerted in the disposition of land once included in the public domain. In 1850, the nation owned 1.4 billion acres, twice the size of its present holdings. In the past 120 years an area equal in size to the entire public domain of today has been transferred from federal ownership to the states, to railroads, to settlers, to speculators, to colleges, and most recently to local governments. The statutes and directives which implemented these dispositions have substantially determined the eventual usage of lands so affected.

Beyond the disposition of lands with strings attached, the federal government today through its myriad programs of domestic public works and subsidies exerts influence over both public and private land-use decisions in a variety of ways. Throughout the country, current land users attempt to preserve the value of their rights by land-use regulation. However, the local regulatory function is far eclipsed by the role of federal programs having a direct and massive impact upon the value and utility of land, such as the reclamation program, the TVA program and its analogues, the rural electrification program, and the federal highway trust fund. In the metropolitan context, perhaps no more profound determinants of urban land-use patterns could be cited than the Federal Housing Administration home mortgage insurance program and the Interstate Highway System. Beyond these a variety of non-fiscal incentives and the complex of federal, state, and local tax structures may change values.

To recognize the importance of the federal government in the contemporary land-use decision process is scarcely to discern any consistent policy or objective towards which federal authority has been directed, whether for good or evil, however. Indeed, for 200 years the only consistency in federal policies and actions with respect to land may be found in their inconsistency. To cite a familiar example, between 1944 and 1964, roughly 22.5 million acres were brought into production through federally assisted reclamation programs. During much of the same period, Congress spent many billions of dollars to *remove* agricultural land from production.

The promulgation and implementation of conflicting policies and programs are, of course, not merely a question of governmental ineptitude. As a pluralistic entity representing a complex societal mosaic of interests and interest-groups, Congress must weigh mutually inconsistent demands, viewpoints, and pressures. Occasionally, it manages to decide in favor of one side or the other. Frequently, however, it attempts to accommodate both interests, at the price of satisfying neither, as for example in the move toward development of an urban land policy in the last decade. The legislation that passed the Senate would have established a national land policy, calling for the States to develop "balanced" land-use plans, protecting the environment and recreational opportunities while providing for economic growth. Yet the perennial challenge reappears. How do we protect ecological interests and still permit necessary urban growth? Already we see the defenders of suburban exclusiveness wrapping them-

selves in the popular bunting of concern for ecology, finding still another
basis for inhibiting the free movement of excluded groups.

Yet in these haltering moves Daniel Bell claims to see a trend in the
United States away from a society based on a private-enterprise market
system toward one in which the most important economic decisions will
be made at the political level in terms of consciously defined "goals" and
"priorities." The question which we must then ask is whether this signals
a new move toward goal-oriented planning in the United States, planning
that focusses on *ends* and uses political power to achieve *means-ends
closure.* In the post-industrial society, Bell says, production and business
decisions will be subordinated to, or will derive from, other forces in
society; the crucial decisions regarding the growth to the economy and
its balance will come from *government,* and they will be based on the
government's sponsorship of research and development, of cost-effective-
ness and cost-benefit analysis. The making of decisions, he says, because
of the intricately linked nature of their consequences, will have an increasingly technical character, involving increasing application of systems
methods and cybernetic procedures. Emergent post-industrial society will
be as different from contemporary urban-industrial society, he concludes,
as was the industrial order from its pre-industrial predecessors. (See
Table 2.)

In short, Bell's argument is that the most important social change of
our time is a process of direct and deliberate contrivance of change itself.
Men, he says, now seek to anticipate change, measure the course of its
direction and its impact, control it, and even shape it for predetermined
ends with a greater chance of success than the big dreamers of the past.
Inevitably, he says, a complex society (like the large complex organizations within it) becomes a planning society. Necessarily, government begins to plan in dealing with such questions as renewal of cities, building
of housing, and planning of medical care. The political order necessarily
becomes the control system of the society. But who runs it, and for whose
(or what) ends? This question is of particular significance, because politics
seldom show men and women at their best.

Ironically, the question was raised by the present incumbent of the
White House when, in 1969, he established a National Goals Research
Staff, with several functions:

a. forecasting future developments, and assessing the longer-range consequences of present social trends,
b. measuring the probable future impact of alternative courses of action,
c. estimating the actual range of social choice, i.e., what goals may be at-
   tainable,
d. developing and maintaining social indicators that can reflect the direction
   and rate of change of American society.

Certainly, no one could quarrel with this venture, the development of
a capability to enable us to assess where we stand and are going with re-

TABLE 2. BELL'S SCHEMA OF SOCIAL CHANGE*

	Pre-Industrial	Industrial	Post-Industrial		
Regions:	Asia Africa Latin America	Western Europe Soviet Union Japan	United States		
Economic sector:	Primary Extractive:	Secondary Goods producing:	Tertiary	Quaternary	Quinary
	Agriculture Mining Fishing Timber	Manufacturing Processing	Transport Recreation	Trade Finance Insurance Real Estate	Health Education Research Government
Occupational structure:	Farmer Miner Fisherman Unskilled worker	Semi-skilled worker Engineer	Professional and technical Scientists		
Technology:	Raw materials	Energy	Information		
Design:	Game against nature	Game against fabricated nature	Game between persons		
Methodology:	Common sense experience	Empiricism Experimentation	Abstract theory: models, simulation, decision theory, systems analysis		
Time perspective:	Orientation to the past Ad hoc responses	Ad hoc adaptiveness Projections	Future orientation Forecasting		
Axial principle:	Traditionalism:	Economic growth:	Centrality of and codification of theoretical knowledge		
	Land/ resource limitation	State or private control of investment decisions			

* *Source:* "General Schema of Social Change," from *The Coming of the Post-Industrial Society,* by Daniel Bell. © 1973 by Daniel Bell. Basic Books, Inc., Publishers, New York.

spect to our values and goals, and to evaluate specific programs and determine their impact. The need is unquestionable—increasingly public officials and elected representatives of varying competence, coming to power through an electoral process that fails to produce choices based on hard criteria about what the goals are and how decisions should be made, do in fact make major decisions in the attempt to change the future states of our social environment.

What variables are taken into account? No behavioral scientist will disagree with the basic role that is played by cognition—the way that the world is perceived to be, in contrast to what it in fact is. We have all been trained to believe that the structure of any system operates on behavior through the mediation of cognition and that structure in its turn is composed of aggregations of behavior called "processes." In other words, *decisions rest on beliefs about facts,* and they successively transform these facts. To the extent that beliefs are erroneous or distorted, errors are made in social strategies that waste resources and create future problems by the change processes they set in motion.

Surely, then, better statistics of direct normative interest should help us make balanced, comprehensive and concise judgments about the condition of society. Surely we can benefit if, as many have said, we "apply real science to social affairs," thus eliminating the corruptions of the principle of rationality that arise when decisions about social affairs are made on the basis of beliefs about facts, rather than "true knowledge."

Surely, *Soviet* cyberneticists have said in that command economy and a massive experiment has been set in motion to test the applicability of cybernetics to total social system transition in the U.S.S.R. Cybernetics has been tied to the goal-seeking activity of a centrally-directed state, linked as a science and technology to the concept of controlled social progress, and ideologically by means of theory of development to the fundamental tenets of communism, in the Unified Information Network of the U.S.S.R., scheduled for completion during the 1970s.

The problems addressed by Soviet cybernetics are exactly those that confront American decision-makers faced by increasing complexity and dynamism of our social system—how to tie together the notions of stability, change, and goal-seeking necessary to the development of post-industrial social systems. But there is an implicit specter of control, and it is this specter that lies at the roots of the failure of public will in the United States in this regard, as evidenced by the termination of the National Goals Research Staff and the subsequent failure of both the Domestic Council and H.U.D. to develop a national growth policy. Stating the issue as baldly as possibly, the about-face reflected in the Domestic Council's 1972 report, *National Growth,* quoted earlier reveals that American society is inherently incapable of being goal-oriented for deep-seated ideological reasons despite Bell's arguments to the contrary. Accordingly, applied cybernetic rationality *cannot* be the basis of new approaches to the planning of American land use, unless there is a change of will that I consider to be most unlikely.

Whatever the other trends may be, pluralism still prevails. Thus, as one commentator remarked recently "no computer-based simulation model jazzed-up analysis scheme is really going to get very far in terms of adoption if the policy-maker has the feeling that he can't control it." The *modus operandi* of our governmental agencies is that the accountable officials should have the decisive role in determining what programs are developed and how money is spent, and they are the officials who must respond to interest-group and political pressures.

Under such pressures, applied rationality as presently and somewhat pretentiously conceived presents fundamental challenges to the traditional and persisting American decision-making style. To cite one example, the politician who remains in power by manipulating interest-group politics and dispensing patronage has no interest in systems planning because it provides a method of decision-making that is more rational than the interest-group politics he seeks to manipulate. Indeed, deliberate fuzziness is what such a politician seeks, a clouding of the issues to enable him to manipulate. In the absence of an agreed-upon direction for society, such clouding may be an alternative technique for survival under conditions of increasing complexity.

The application of cybernetic techniques serves, in American society, to intensify the individual's feelings of anxiety and uncertainty—witness the current discussion of the privacy issue—even though it can help him cope with the barriers to understanding in data-glutted circumstances. Thus, nationwide computerized real estate services do make executive home-seeking much easier. But the vast majority are not receptive to cybernetic techniques, actively opposing them or having a fixed and limited Bunker-esque view of exactly what information is legitimate and useful. At the same time, many of our current national problems result from the conflict between the policy-maker's sense of potential power to generate and implement better policies based on more information, and his sense of vulnerability to exposure of personal and organizational insufficiencies. Thus, there is little interest in monitoring or assessing public programs because the evaluation may show other than overwhelming success. As one of my colleagues said recently, "I often feel that politicians don't want issues crystallized. There's a certain kind of defense mechanism that operates in avoiding the crystallization of issues that would conflict and sharpen when they get crystallized." More information would only be used by other groups to challenge the policy-maker's policies and programs.

Toward Policy Alternatives

Where, then, do we stand? Conceptual advances in the social sciences in recent decades correspond in direction to similar advances in the physical and biological sciences, pointing to a view of reality as interdependent, irrevocable process. What, then, might any reasonable rational man agree is needed to ensure that changing societies make wise decisions about land use? There are perhaps four interacting ingredients:

1. *Information.* Information is needed to tell us what our society is like now, how rapidly and in what ways it is changing, and what scientific and technological alternatives to present practices exist or can be found.

2. *Social analysis.* Analysis is needed to determine what relations exist between current actions and future effects, to weigh the merits of alternative priority systems, to derive practical, achievable goals for society, and to determine how best to allocate our finite resources to attain those goals.

3. *Well-informed decision-makers.* Society requires mechanisms to ensure that decision-makers, including the public, have access to the information they need, have available the results of the analyses carried out, and have alternative courses of action formulated for their consideration.

4. *Appropriate institutions.* Institutions are needed to ensure that decisions can be put into practice. They take many forms—political, financial, legal, and educational.

But to say that is to simply state truisms. Is there perhaps a basis for acting within such an informational framework, recognizing the continuing significance of American pluralism, and utilizing the mainstream means of determining land use, while simultaneously producing land-use patterns that are different from those obtaining today? The skeleton of such an analysis is clear if, from economic theory, we adopt three axioms: (1) individual self-interest underlies human behavior; (2) prices act as signals guiding this behavior; and (3) trade-offs—more elaborately, decisions derived from cost-benefit analyses—can be steered by suitable management of prices. This set of assumptions permits, in principle, the implementation of an optimal allocation of resources within the free market.

Let us then admit that there are unaccounted-for negative externalities, as well as the windfall-wipeout problem and the bearing of costs by consumers rather than producers. How does one internalize these externalities so that the logic of existing land-use patterns reflects more accurately the total array of costs and benefits associated with land-use interdependencies? When one considers the difficulty of enforcing most forms of regulation, it becomes clear that only so-called "shadow prices" by which individuals and firms pay for the negative externalities they *impose* on others will work. The clearest case is that of environmental pollution, in which such shadow prices are called effluent residuals charges. These residuals charges are designed to raise the costs of discharging harmful wastes to the environment, to lead to the curbing of the discharges and ultimately to a reduction of the damages caused, thus extending the corrective powers of the market to the commons. The requirement that environmental impact statements be prepared is one step on the way to developing such residuals charges if effluents are not eliminated at the source.

Although we have been less eager to acknowledge the fact, the ideas developed in the environmental area apply to the misallocation of *human* resources within our metropolitan systems as well, and in turn suggest new approaches to urban land-use policy that adequately represent a range of social concerns.

Starting from predilections for individual choice and marketplace economics in which consumers can purchase exactly as much as they want of different goods and services, most economic writers have gravitated to the notion that the smaller the social group involved in making a social choice the better its decision is likely to be. The validity of this notion rests on two assumptions: (1) that members of small groups can more easily and cheaply carry on negotiations and achieve compromises than can members of large groups, and (2) that the existence of many small groups makes it possible for the groups, as collective decision-makers, to achieve homogeneity as to tastes and preferences among members of the respective groups, and relatively easy shifting of locations in a mobile society to ensure that homogeneity is maintained as individuals move along occupational career trajectories and through the life cycle.

Following this logic, Charles Tiebout developed his now-classic "pure theory of local expenditures." He concluded that choice-making in metropolitan areas has been furthered by the approximation of a market situation through maintaining numerous municipal jurisdictions, each competing for residents by offering them packages of amenities and public goods with price tags in the form of taxes. With numerous jurisdictions to choose from, Tiebout argued that each household or firm can select the community where the division of consumption between public and private, and the mix of public goods, most closely fits its own preferences. Voting by foot thus complements the workings of the invisible hand as a means of adjusting the social-economic process to the wants and needs of consumers. Such an argument assumes that there will be communities of residents with fairly homogeneous interests and preferences, which further implies a homogeneity of income. The model thus implies segregation according to economic class.

It is perfectly clear that such segregation has developed and increased as metropolitan areas have grown. The market mechanism has been operating. But it is also clear that to the extent it is valid, the Tiebout thesis respecting the *benefits* of multiple jurisdictions applies only to middle- and upper-class households, who have the greatest mobility and resources, and exercise preemptive choices with respect to both locations and amenities. Low-income groups bear most of the costs of upper-income preemptions, having no latitude for movement, lacking mobility and options. Choice-making has been the prerogative of higher-income groups, who play exclusionary politics to deny the foot-vote and the efficiency of market mechanisms to lower income groups. One result is ghettoization of the poor in the oldest and most polluted of the least desirable inner-city locations, imposing a far greater health burden on them. Moreover, the limitations upon choice in ghetto neighborhoods further imply growing social pathologies that sweep out and impose costs on all—costs of welfare, of crime control, and the like. The availability of multiple jurisdictions that maximize choice for the privileged thus ignores the external consequences imposed upon those denied such choice, especially where communities opt for particular types and qualities of services by exclusionary devices such as land-use zoning that restrict those with the greatest public service needs to other locations.

Federal policies have been of little help, instead providing more options for the affluent while compounding the ghettoization of the poor in high-rise public housing to create a complex of problems, a "mess." The long-term compounding of accumulative deprivation in the underclass is now coming home to roost. We need only cite the increasing panic in suburban America about rising crime rates, and the fixation upon law and order.

What follows from the above is that there is a need for imposing residual charges that raise the costs of denying freedom of choice to low- and semi-skilled Americans, to produce a curbing of the constraints on choice, and ultimately a reduction in the damages caused by the denial—thus extending the corrective powers of the market by changing the community concept of self interest. And by analogy with the environmental impact statement, a broader range of considerations can be introduced into land-use decisions on the human side by use of relocation impact statements and housing impact statements.

The crux of what we are talking about on the social side is housing patterns in relation to job locations. As Whitney Young reminded us, it gets clearer and clearer that whether we are talking about education, health, welfare, employment, or any other element of community stability, the central factor is housing. And this means more than the quality of housing, although that is very important. It is also *where* the housing is, which means the land-use pattern.

Noting the externalities involved, the Commission on Population Growth and the American Future has noted, "while the absence in the suburbs of an adequate supply of low- and moderate-income housing available to all races is certainly not the sole or even the primary cause of unemployment or underemployment in the central city, it is a contributing factor which needs to be remedied." Recognizing this, the Equal Employment Opportunity Commission issued a draft memorandum in 1970 (subsequently withdrawn under fire) arguing that relocation of a business is a *prima facie* violation of Title VII of the Civil Rights Act of 1964 if: (1) the community from which the plant is moved has a higher percentage of minority workers than the new location, or (2) the transfer is more detrimental to minority workers than to others, and (3) the employer fails to take measures to correct the "disparate effect." This last point is important, because it implies that the relocation had the foreseeable effect of excluding minority groups from employment. The burden of proof would be on the employer, since relocation to an area with few minority residents would result in recruiting practices that favor the local labor market, and thus decrease the chance for minority group employment. "Unless an employer makes special efforts to institute a minority recruiting program," the memo states, "he will have failed in his duty of fair recruitment."

In all cases in the Equal Employment Opportunity Commission's scheme, the employer would have been required to prove business *necessity*, not just convenience. If he moved a plant to a suburb because land costs are lower, he would have to prove that there are no other areas available that would give minority workers better employment opportunities. Finally, the memo suggested a plan to assure a continual supply of minority labor by: (1) instituting special recruitment efforts in the nearest areas of minority residence; and (2) assuring minority workers the same access to the employer's facilities that nonminorities enjoy. As the draft memorandum noted:

> If commuting expenses for minorities are high, they should be paid. If commuting is impossible, housing arrangements should be made: the employer should provide moving expenses. If necessary, he should also provide or assist in the search for housing and use legal and commercial leverage to assure housing opportunities for minorities

and (3) establishing a goal for minority employment, the same as he presumably set at the original location, based on the minority population ratio of the original community.

Such is a statement of corporate responsibility, imposing, if you like, residuals charges for human resource degradation on American business. What of community responsibility? Is the analogy with spillover effects in pollution valid in this case, too?

There are several initiatives that bear examination. Proceeding from the notion that the community as a whole should begin to bear the cost of housing the poor, Dayton, Ohio, has the Miami Valley "fair share" plan for low- and moderate-income housing involving each community in the metropolitan area, and a similar effort is being sparked by Chicago's Leadership Council. I think we have reason to question whether fair share agreements will ever work, however, in the absence of a stick that only can be brought to bear either by corporate America in its own self-interest, or by the federal government. There is too much scope for a community to be a laggard—to let other more liberal communities bear the brunt—because laggardliness does not cost them anything. Rather, to achieve individual benefits, they impose costs on the others. It is for this reason that we must seek land-use patterns that, while maintaining an essential freedom of choice, properly internalize the social costs of that choice at the source. Only by establishing new values for the rights that accompany land ownership will land-use patterns develop that are more socially and environmentally responsible than these obtaining today.

I am indebted to S. Golant, D. G. Hagman, C. L. Harriss, D. Jones and J. Meltzer for their comments. R. H. Platt, Jr. was kind enough to permit me to draw on an essay of his concerning the federal role in U. S. land use. But needless to say, all responsibility for opinions expressed, for errors and for confusion remain mine.

Index

About The American Assembly

The American Assembly was established by Dwight D. Eisenhower at Columbia University in 1950. It holds nonpartisan meetings and publishes authoritative books to illuminate issues of United States policy.

An affiliate of Columbia, with offices in the Graduate School of Business, the Assembly is a national educational institution incorporated in the State of New York.

The Assembly seeks to provide information, stimulate discussion, and evoke independent conclusions in matters of vital public interest.

AMERICAN ASSEMBLY SESSIONS

At least two national programs are initiated each year. Authorities are retained to write background papers presenting essential data and defining the main issues in each subject.

About sixty men and women representing a broad range of experience, competence, and American leadership meet for several days to discuss the Assembly topic and consider alternatives for national policy.

All Assemblies follow the same procedure. The background papers are sent to participants in advance of the Assembly. The Assembly meets in small groups for four or five lengthy periods. All groups use the same agenda. At the close of these informal sessions, participants adopt in plenary session a final report of findings and recommendations.

Regional, state, and local Assemblies are held following the national session at Arden House. Assemblies have also been in England, Switzerland, Malaysia, Canada, the Caribbean, South America, Central America, the Philippines, and Japan. Over one hundred institutions have co-sponsored one or more Assemblies.

ARDEN HOUSE

Home of The American Assembly and scene of the national sessions is Arden House, which was given to Columbia University in 1950 by W. Averell Harriman. E. Roland Harriman joined his brother in contributing toward adaptation of the property for conference purposes. The buildings and surrounding land, known as the Harriman Campus of Columbia University, are fifty miles north of New York City.

Arden House is a distinguished conference center. It is self-supporting and operates throughout the year for use by organizations with educational objectives.

AMERICAN ASSEMBLY BOOKS

The background papers for each Assembly program are published in cloth and paperbound editions for use by individuals, libraries, businesses, public agencies, nongovernmental organizations, educational institutions, discussion and service groups. In this way the deliberations of Assembly sessions are continued and extended.

The subjects of Assembly programs to date are:

1951——United States–Western Europe Relationships
1952——Inflation
1953——Economic Security for Americans
1954——The United States' Stake in the United Nations
——The Federal Government Service
1955——United States Agriculture
——The Forty-Eight States
1956——The Representation of the United States Abroad
——The United States and the Far East
1957——International Stability and Progress
——Atoms for Power
1958——The United States and Africa
——United States Monetary Policy
1959——Wages, Prices, Profits, and Productivity
——The United States and Latin America
1960——The Federal Government and Higher Education
——The Secretary of State
——Goals for Americans
1961——Arms Control: Issues for the Public
——Outer Space: Prospects for Man and Society
1962——Automation and Technological Change
——Cultural Affairs and Foreign Relations
1963——The Population Dilemma
——The United States and the Middle East
1964——The United States and Canada
——The Congress and America's Future
1965——The Courts, the Public, and the Law Explosion
——The United States and Japan
1966——State Legislatures in American Politics
——A World of Nuclear Powers?
——The United States and the Philippines
——Challenges to Collective Bargaining
1967——The United States and Eastern Europe
——Ombudsmen for American Government?
1968——Uses of the Seas
——Law in a Changing America
——Overcoming World Hunger
1969——Black Economic Development
——The States and the Urban Crisis
1970——The Health of Americans
——The United States and the Caribbean

1971——The Future of American Transportation
——Public Workers and Public Unions
1972——The Future of Foundations
——Prisoners in America
1973——The Worker and the Job
——Choosing the President
1974——Land Use
——The Future of Museums
——The Transnational Corporation

Second Editions, Revised:

1962——The United States and the Far East
1963——The United States and Latin America
——The United States and Africa
1964——United States Monetary Policy
1965——The Federal Government Service
——The Representation of the United States Abroad
1968——Cultural Affairs and Foreign Relations
——Outer Space: Prospects for Man and Society
1969——The Population Dilemma
1972——The Congress and America's Future